HEALING RACISM IN AMERICA

Healing Racism In America
A Prescription For The Disease

by

Nathan Rutstein

Design by Chester Makoski, Jr.

Library of Congress Catalogue No: 92-63009

ISBN 0-9633007-1-7

Table Of Contents

Acknowledgements

This book is essentially a sequel to *To Be One: A Battle Against Racism*, which was an autobiographical account of how I discovered my latent racist feelings, and what I did to try to overcome them.

But *Healing Racism* is more than a description of the continuation of my personal struggle. It is a sharing of what I have learned about the disease of racism in the past four years, and, more importantly, what I have discovered to be a vaccine against this pernicious malady that continues to prevent America from fulfilling its potential as a truly great democracy.

My search and effort to convey in print what I found was aided by a number of people across America and elsewhere. Before mentioning who they are, I want to point out that my basic under-standing of the disease of racism stems from the guidance I received from the sacred writings of the Bahá'í faith. Without their profound influence, my allies and I would never have discovered the healing process that we believe can, in one or two generations, wipe out racism in America.

The founders of the Houston Institute for the Healing of Racism were the source of great inspiration to me. Their courage and devotion to a noble cause – the eradication of racism and the unifying of mankind – helped to sustain my efforts in the race relations field. Ours has been a synergistic relationship. I will never forget them: Elisa Brown, Jackie Cone, Barbara Hacker, Andre'nea King, Freddie and Kim Polk, Cherry Steinwender, Mikal Rasheed, Sharon Davis, Nelson Brignoni, Barbara Inihara, Roy and Shiva Lee, Zhiani Hedayati, and Martha Ungamootoo.

I have also been inspired by the hundreds of other Institute members I have met in my travels, who, despite opposition from conservative and liberal skeptics and doomsayers, persevered, and are today part of Institutes successfully engaged in healing the infected and wounded victims of racism. Today, their services are being sought by police departments, corporations, schools, health departments, churches and universities.

One group occupies a special place in my heart. They are seven elderly black and white women from Citrus County, Florida, who invited me down to help them form an Institute for the Healing of Racism. They all shared the same vision, possessed the enthusiasm of teenagers and the determination to succeed in their social development project. What they were doing, they believed, was an act of worship.

It is important to note that the race unity workshops done by my wife, Carol, and Bette Roberts, an Amherst, Massachusetts, elementary school teacher, helped to stimulate my interest in finding a solution to the black-white conflict in America. I also benefited from Carol's continual research on racial issues.

In my quest to gain a clinical understanding of the nature of the disease of racism, I received valuable help from Dr. John Woodall, a psychiatrist associated with Harvard University Medical School, and Dr. Robert Davenport, a pastoral counselor in Annapolis, Maryland.

Grace Bates, Dr. Phyllis Gudger-Porter, Sherlock Haynes, Thelma Khelgahti, Abena King, and Karen Streets-Anderson provided me with precious insights on the nature of the wounds that afflict African-Americans.

My historical research was aided by long conversations with Tod Rutstein, a social science teacher at Baltimore Friends School, and Bernard Streets, a race relations lecturer and noted microbiologist based in Manchester, New Hampshire. Further historical insights were gained from Professor John Bracey of the University of Massachusetts at Amherst, and Professor Richard Thomas of Michigan State University.

The continual encouragement and insightful feedback of Whitcomb Publishing's president, Paul Robbins, made it possible for me to meet our manuscript completion deadline. Also valuable were the research efforts and pre-production work of Jennifer Garvin.

I'm also indebted to the wonderful work done by cover artist Chester Makoski and Whitcomb's production director, Craig Harmsen.

Foreword

The first time I can remember hearing something terribly unpleasant that turned out to be a profound truth in disguise was when I was seventeen. Ruth Hampson, a lovely senior woman I knew in my community, was giving a talk on "The Thing That Unites Us." Buffeted by the division and turmoil of the 1960s, I was anxious to hear a healing message from someone I loved and respected. Something within me eagerly sought some definitive statement that there was cause for hope in a world torn by violence and despair. My soul needed this like one sick with fever needs a soothing balm; like a lost child needs the way home. Ruth would surely deliver.

The friendly greeting and obligatory hot tea at Ruth's house belied the bitter Chicago cold as I settled into one of those couches that embrace you as you work your way down into it.

Ruth began to speak with her familiar sweetness that assured us we were all her closest friends. Anyone who happened to be in that room genuinely was.

There was space in Ruth's heart for everyone, with room to spare; but the living room that day was packed. Ruth spoke simply and straight to the point:

"There are a variety of experiences that unite us as a human family. But the one I feel is most important is the experience of anguish."

This was not what I wanted to hear.

A reflex rebelled inside, "No, that can't be!" Then the reason, "I'm trying to get away from pain." I'd seen enough of it. Then, the desired solution, "Tell me about love, compassion or hope, but not anguish!"

In a paradoxical way, my history of pain was preventing me from acknowledging the simple truth that pain is ubiquitous. To state this truth is not an endorsement of pain or to wish it on anyone. It's just true: All people have experienced anguish.

What Ruth knew was something I have come to understand in the past twenty years. Life presents us with pain; some we cause ourselves and some we have no control over. Regardless, we are presented with a choice. Pain can be turned to bitterness and despair, or it can be the root of our compassion and desire to ease the pain of others. The former response has fear at its base, a fear that we cannot find a way out of our pain. The latter springs from a deep and abiding sense of the strength and beauty of the human spirit we all share, a sense that embraces all that life offers – its pain and pleasure, its follies and triumph.

Ruth had that sense. That's why she could speak of anguish with the same acceptance she spoke of love. Her powerful love of life embraced and harnessed life's anguish into a force for compassion and mutual healing.

Nat Rutstein is like that, too. He can talk about the pain of racism because he is no longer afraid of it. And more, he believes that people can naturally rise up to a higher vision of life that includes all people, and in so doing, find a way out of the anguish of the racism that corrupts and corrodes the spirit of our nation.

The alienation and anguish of racism have engendered very subtle degrees of denial that have devastating effects on the growth of relations between ethnic groups. Nat has decided to tackle this issue head-on.

He tells us something unpleasant, but true. Racism is a disease and a wound and we are all affected in one way or another by virtue of growing up in this society. He doesn't say this to incite or to blame, but as a call to the principles we hold most dear as Americans. He says it because he feels there is a way out – but only if we speak honestly and with compassion.

What Nat has done is a remarkable example of the power of principled action. With no particular expertise, but a profound drive to live the truth, Nat has turned a personal conviction into a national, and, now, international movement. And he has done this in a way that endows each of us with the knowledge that little more is required than a commitment to the principle of the oneness of humanity, perseverance and patience.

It is no overstatement to say that the destiny of America hangs in the balance over the issue of how we live as a multi-ethnic society. Not only are the founding principles of the country – liberty, equality and justice – in the balance, but the world as a whole cries out for a vindication of these principles in establishing that a diverse society can live in peace. The Institutes for the Healing of Racism, then, fit into a larger global movement toward finding means for diverse peoples to live in unity.

The safe atmosphere created in the Institute, like the friendship, hot tea and ease of relating in Ruth's house, makes it possible to discuss any topics without feeling threatened. Even difficult truths in one's own life can be healed, and can become the impetus for shared growth.

There have been and will continue to be critics who say the Institutes for the Healing of Racism are academically unsophisticated. But the time for words from the Ivory Tower are long past. Scholars must get into the action and be worthy critics and contributors. Nat has thrown himself head first into the most challenging social issue facing the country, with little regard for the personal cost.

The Institute's format is open enough to allow for growth and experimentation. Expert critics could best use their energies from the inside, in the trenches, helping to develop the Institute, or movements like the Institutes for the Healing of Racism, to help spread their influence.

Readers can take heart that, with over one hundred Institutes for the Healing of Racism in existence, a network is in place into which their efforts can be channeled. We no longer need to feel powerless in the face of racism. We can, and we must, do something about it.

We owe Nat Rutstein a great deal for his courage and spirit. Now we can read for ourselves his blueprint for getting about the business of binding up the nation's wounds and building a truly united America.

JOHN WOODALL, M.D.
HARVARD UNIVERSITY
CAMBRIDGE, MASSACHUSETTS

Preface

As I was writing this book, the verdict in the Rodney King case triggered a racial explosion in Los Angeles that killed and injured more people and gutted more homes and businesses than the previous race riot in that city twenty-seven years ago. This time, the burning and looting and killing extended beyond the black ghetto.

While most of us were horrified by the fury and brutality expressed by the rioters, we couldn't help but wonder if the race relations progress seemingly made since the 1960s might be a mirage. Certainly, most blacks feel that way.

It was obvious that the rage, bitterness and hopelessness that existed in Watts in 1965 still exist there. The only difference is that a new generation of women and men are crying out for freedom, for respect, for an opportunity to attain the kind of security that most white Americans enjoy. Actually, the cry of today's African-Americans is not much different than the cry of their ancestors who came to the "New World" in chains about four hundred years ago. True, they are no longer slaves, but they have yet to win their freedom.

What happened in Los Angeles can occur in hundreds of cities and towns across America, because the social and economic conditions are similar. The wounds sustained decades ago remain deep and continue to fester.

Interestingly, the reaction to the latest Los Angeles race riot was very much like the reaction to Watts. Troops were dispatched to quell the unrest; government officials and religious leaders called for programs that would rebuild the area, create jobs, and provide improved medical treatment, better educational facilities and opportunities for the residents of the stricken area.

The trouble is that, even if the politicians keep their promises, the underlying cause of the latest Los Angeles race riot won't be addressed. Even the news media refuse to zero in on the root cause of the problem.

In reality, a heavy infusion of federal funds into South Central Los Angeles will be an exercise in buying peace. The idea is that the more money you invest, the longer the peace will last. Undoubtedly, the social and economic programs that are established will dull the pain. But more than anesthesia is required. Because the United States is the largest debtor nation in the world, Los Angeles can't expect a constant supply of federal funds. After the shock of the riot wears off, the outpouring will be reduced to a trickle. And then what?

While the money is needed, it is important to note that dollars alone can't bring about what African-Americans, not only in Los Angeles, but everywhere in America, are crying out for.

Los Angeles Mayor Tom Bradley knows that money alone is not the answer:

"If we as a nation continue to ignore the racial reality of our times, tiptoe around it, demagogue it or flee from it, we're going to pay an enormous price. Maybe out of this horrible set of events that's saddened me terribly will come some healing, some coming together, some commitment."

This book is an answer to Mayor Bradley's plea. It reveals how to heal, how to bring people together and how to get women and men, whites and people of color, committed to overcoming, once and for all, racism, *which is the most challenging issue confronting America today.*

What is offered is a concept that has been tried, and, because of its rate of success, is gaining momentum. To appreciate the concept, it is important that everyone become acquainted with the gravity of the race problem in America. This book does that, revealing information that some readers may find offensive, unpatriotic, even painful. It may even shake some people's religious faith.

Rest assured, it is not my intention to hurt anyone's feelings. I know that being exposed to the truth can be a painful experience, especially if what you learn contradicts what you always believed was true. I must admit that in my search I was shaken and angered by what I found. But my rage has subsided. Now, I don't regret being outraged and shamed by what I discovered, because it was a catalyst to my becoming committed to healing the disease of racism and becoming involved in the worthy service of unifying mankind.

While events like the Los Angeles race riots still make my blood boil, my understanding of why such eruptions occur keeps me focused on my commitment. I don't despair, but rather, redouble my efforts. Witnessing blacks and whites who once hated each other learning to love one another is the fuel that keeps me going.

1
Search for a Cure

Ever since *To Be One* was published in the autumn of 1988, I have found myself deeply involved in America's race issue, not as a highly touted race relations expert, nor as a much heralded activist. It wasn't something I longed to do; a set of circumstances drew me into the struggle.

Because of my book's impact on both blacks and whites, many people have approached me for answers to questions that had been plaguing them for a long time. Evidently they have felt they could trust me, since *To Be One* was an autobiographical account of how I discovered the infection of racism within me, and my search for a cure. Not having the answers at the time, I suddenly found myself an explorer of the disease's origins and symptoms. The more knowledge I gained, the more opportunities I had to help heal others. Interestingly, that process has been personally rewarding; for in trying to heal others I found myself being healed. While I have learned a great deal in the past three years, and may have helped to heal some folks, I'm sure I have much more to learn, which, I pray, will help me become a more effective healer of the victims of racism I meet in the future – both the infected and the wounded. (The pathology of this social disease will be described later on, as will the nature of the wound.)

One thing I have learned from my trips across America is that the pain and frustration that racism generated in the past still exist, despite the passage of good civil rights legislation, the adoption of affirmative action policies and the creation of multicultural educational programs. And it isn't only people of color who are hurting, but also well-meaning whites who recognize their infection and grope aimlessly, at times frantically, for a remedy. Even those who aren't seeking a remedy, who believe their racist attitudes are justified, are hurting; for living day after day with unreleased anger and hatred is painful.

In many respects, the racial condition in America and Europe is worse than in the 1960s, when Dr. Martin Luther King, Jr. was spearheading a crusade to end racial segregation and discrimination. This is evidenced by the polarization of today's African-American community, a polarization that is more pronounced than it was in the 1960s, when many blacks sensed they had, at last, reached the threshold of social equality. Some even felt they were approaching the "Promised Land." Today, many blacks view that time of great promise as a mirage, as a cruel hoax; they no longer share Dr. King's dream of racial unity in America, which he revealed to the world on the steps of the Lincoln Memorial in Washington, D.C., in 1963. Their initial impulse is to avoid – as much as possible – relationships with whites, for they no longer can tolerate being rejected, even in a subtle way. Nor can they tolerate being on the receiving end of a patronizing attitude. It doesn't matter how sweet or well-intentioned the perpetrator is. Blacks are tired of always having to be on guard to repulse disrespectful actions on the part of the people who have oppressed them for so long. They are tired of always taking the first step to build bridges of understanding between the white and black communities – that never result in meaningful changes. They are tired of pretending to be what they are not. They are tired of always being accepting of what white folks say. They are tired of having to say "yes" when they want to say "no." They are tired of being tools of tokenism. They now look back and cry out to themselves, and to those they trust: "What good did all of our sacrifices in the sixties accomplish – when the pain we felt then, we feel now?"

This feeling prevails even though all racial barriers have officially been removed from public facilities. Blacks are now mayors of some of America's biggest cities; a black sits on the highest court of the land;

President Bush appointed a black physician to serve as secretary of health and human services; a black physicist heads the National Science Foundation; and in baseball the president of the National League is an African-American. There are black congressmen and women, police chiefs, sheriffs and corporate CEOs; the country's top military officer is a black; some of the leading television personalities are African-Americans; and more black males are making more than $25,000 a year than ever before. While those facts may impress a foreign visitor or a white American who has been sheltered from the gravity of the racism problem in his country, many blacks know that the atmosphere that breeds racism has changed little since their nation came into being. What was won in the sixties was an opportunity to gain a closer look at the privileges whites enjoy. And this has only intensified the frustration and anger in the black community.

Mervin Aubespin, a black who is associate editor for development at the Louisville Courier-Journal, said, during a visit to St. Michael's College in Vermont in 1991, that racism "is everywhere I go."

"Racism is worse now in this country than any time I can remember," he said. Aubespin marched with Dr. King from Selma to Montgomery in the 1960s.

Not the abolition of slavery, the outlawing of Jim Crowism, the Civil Rights Movement of the sixties, not even the sacrifices made by black and white martyrs of the human rights cause in the past 150 years, have been able to change the atmosphere – that like fertilizer keeps the twisted tree of racism bearing bitter fruit.

What many blacks see when they check out their community's present-day condition many whites avoid taking to heart, for it doesn't directly affect them. What they know is based on what they see on television or read in the newspaper – information that usually aggravates their infection and reinforces their deep-rooted feelings that blacks are inherently inferior to whites.

African-Americans must deal with the facts that *twice* as many blacks commit suicide as whites (in the 1950s suicide among blacks was practically unheard of); that black males under forty-five are *ten*

3

times more likely than whites to die from hypertension; that there are more black males in prison than attend college; that *twenty-five percent* of all black males between twenty and twenty-nine years old are either in jail, on parole or on probation; that the incarceration rate among blacks in America is greater than the incarceration rate of South African blacks; that more black males earn less than $5,000 a year than ever before in modern times; that in 1990, *33.9 percent* of conventional mortgage applications filed by blacks with banks and savings and loan associations were denied (the rate of denial for whites was 14.4 percent); that *sixty percent* of all black families are headed by a single parent; that about *eighty percent* of the black children born in America's major cities are born out of wedlock; that *half* of all black children live in poverty; that *twice* as many blacks are unemployed as whites; that *63.3 percent* of all black youngsters still attend segregated schools, and many of those who attend officially integrated schools end up in segregated classes through the tracking process; that more than *fifty percent* of black males drop out of high school; that black-on-black violence is on the rise; that *more than half* of the black community has no health insurance; that the incidence of cancer, heart disease, diabetes and hypertension is much higher among blacks than whites; that blacks have the highest cancer death rate of any group in America; that *sixty-nine percent* of black babies are too poor to receive inoculations against diseases like measles and diphtheria; that black infants are *twice* as likely as white infants to die before their first birthdays; and that in Harlem, the average black male's life span is less than his counterpart in Bangladesh, one of the poorest countries in the world. According to the 1988 Committee on Cities report, there is "greater despair, less hope and less opportunity to escape from poverty and misery among blacks now than in the '60s."

An underclass has emerged in the African-American community that is growing in size and anger. Cut off from the mainstream of America, it has created its own set of mores, laws, and economies, one

4

of which – drugs – has caught the attention of the nation's leadership, but only because its tentacles are reaching into the mainstream of the nation.

When asked during a TV program hosted by Bill Moyers to project what a black teenager in the inner city can expect of the future, prominent American sociologist William Julius Wilson, himself black, said, "I would say your chances in life are rather limited. Unfortunately, you will experience persistent poverty; you will have very little chance of getting a higher-paying job; you will very likely end up having a child out of wedlock, because the men in your community are not marriageable – that is, they experience long-term joblessness; your children are likely to be attending schools where they are not being properly educated, schools that are overwhelmingly impoverished. So your long-term prospects are rather dim.

"I can take you to any inner-city hospital and go to a ward where newborn babies are and predict with high probability where these kids are going to end up in life. Most of them will end up living in poverty, trapped in the inner city. When you can make such predictions, you're talking about a very unfair society."

While many blacks are gravitating toward separatism, many white liberals are expressing concern – some even alarm – over the rush toward separatism in the black community. They appeal for patience.

Political scientist Andrew Hacker raises questions of fairness and justice when he says: "White America continues to ask of its black citizens an extra patience and perseverance that whites have never required of themselves." He is quoted in a *Newsweek* article (March 23, 1992) titled, "Apartheid: American Style."

The invisible and poisonous atmosphere of racism encompasses the entire nation, even those areas where slavery and Jim Crowism never existed, even in a state that has the reputation of being one of the more socially progressive states in America. In Dubuque, Iowa, a racial explosion occurred in 1991 when the City Council adopted a plan to attract one hundred black families in hopes of adding diversity to the virtually all-white city of fifty-eight thousand people. Ku Klux Klan-type cross burnings were sighted across the city; racist graffiti were scrawled on school buildings and churches. An anti-black organization called the National Association for the Advancement of White People established a chapter in the city, attracting a fairly large number of youth and young adults. A chapter of the Ku Klux Klan was also formed. Men and women who never before aired their race prejudice in public pronounced their opposition to the council's diversity plan by resorting to ugly racial epithets in the streets.

As for those few blacks already living in Dubuque? They found themselves trying to cope, as their forefathers did, in what their parents and grandparents had told them were "the more difficult times."

Was what occurred in Dubuque an unnatural social phenomenon? Dr. Joe Feagin, University of Florida sociologist and race relations expert, doesn't think so, according to the New York Times.

"... if in a heartland city with no history of slavery and segregation, you find such virulent racism, it suggests that it is a cancer affecting us all," he said during an interview.

My sense is that most white Americans won't accept Dr. Feagin's observation – and that includes the nation's leaders as well as the average white person. For Americans have a tendency to become defensive or put a positive spin on facts that might embarrass their local community or the nation. Some would accuse Dr. Feagin of being a traitor, anti-American. Others would charge him with being unfair, pointing with pride to the race relations advancements made in the past, especially in the 1960s. And many would recoil with anger at the idea that racism is a disease, and that they may be infected. As a consequence they would retreat into the cocoon of denial. This would be especially true among those whites who view themselves as progressive and liberal-minded – who unwittingly hurt people of color with their patronizing attitude and subconscious air of superiority.

This kind of reaction is precisely the reason why so many blacks don't want anything to do with white liberals. The pain inflicted by a hypocrite, they feel, is more severe than the epithet unleashed by an admitted bigot. "At least with a bigot," many blacks contend, "you know what to expect."

In the mid-1960s, Malcolm X predicted that racism would be overcome in the South sooner than in the North, because, to deal with it, Northern whites must first overcome their delusion they are not prejudiced. Southern whites, on the other hand, must deal only with their prejudice, which they freely acknowledge.

Now, I don't mean to convey the notion that all American whites are evil. Most of them are opposed to racism as an ideology and are people of good will who want to say and do the right thing. But they have their limits when it comes to associating with blacks. The barriers arise when a daughter brings home her black boyfriend; when a black family wants to buy the house next door; when a white is asked to visit someone in a black neighborhood; when a black co-worker gets the promotion a white person wants.

Even many whites, who actively promote human rights causes and may have marched with Dr. King in Selma, Alabama, are carriers of the disease of racism and don't know it. Certainly, if they'd had a choice in the matter, they would have opted not to become infected. But they didn't have a choice. I believe that in most cases white Americans are infected when, as infants, they take their first breath.

As I will explain in greater detail later on, the United States of America was founded by men who believed that people of color were inherently inferior to whites. They created a collective consciousness, from which institutions were born, that reflected their racial views: Schools, courts, legislative bodies, businesses, the arts and sports, and even churches were infected.

Most white Americans equate racism with the activities of the Ku Klux Klan, the Skinheads or neo-Nazis who direct acts of violence at people of color. They don't realize that the disease manifests itself in more subtle ways, in the form of an attitude that triggers behavior they deem natural.

For example, a store clerk suspects black children of wanting to steal candy, but is confident that white children only want to buy candy. Another example: A black family and a white family both move and enroll their children in a desegregated school. Previous school records have not yet arrived. The guidance counselor puts the white child in upper track classes and the black child in lower.

Now, the counselor and the store clerk are not cruel people. Some of them may consider themselves politically progressive. Yet, their actions toward blacks reflect a prejudice that they may not be conscious of. They have been programmed to feel and behave in a certain way when in the presence of blacks. Their inherent and subconscious feeling of superiority toward African-Americans kicks in.

The pollution of racism blankets the entire nation, and the reason most white people don't see it is that they are the pollutant-carriers and producers – and they either don't know it, or don't want to believe that they are.

T he knowledge I gained during the past three years led to an understanding of the racism issue, from which a sensitivity was developed toward the oppressed that I didn't have when I completed *To Be One*. What was in my head moved into my heart. The purpose of this book is to share with the reader what I gained, and what I'm doing with that knowledge.

I now know that unifying humankind is dependent on men and women understanding and internalizing the principle of the oneness of humankind; that there is a difference between prejudice and racism; that the Civil Rights Movement in the sixties was able to eliminate some of the effects of racism, but failed to eradicate the cause; that the black-white issue requires the greatest attention in solving the racism problem; that racism is basically a spiritual problem; that the church – black and white – has failed as a bridge-builder between the races; that education has inadvertently promulgated racism; that denial plagues blacks as well as whites; and that if no way is found to resolve the black-white conflict, an African-American rebellion will erupt across the land – and this time no one will be safe. There are already signs of that happening. In the Los Angeles rioting in the spring of 1992, the burning and looting extended to the suburbs as well as the black community.

What I learned during the past three years wasn't only from black and white academics. I gained as much or even more from inner-city blacks I grew to know; from individuals in the African-American Muslim community; from bewildered school officials groping for solutions to their problems with racism in the classroom; and from beleaguered NAACP officials trying to break down the invisible discrimination barriers in communities reputed to be socially progressive. I learned that racial unity cannot be realized without healing taking place. Fortunately, some of what I have learned has been put to constructive use. It has led to the creation of materials that individuals and communities can use to heal the disease and wounds of racism. After reading *To Be One*, a close friend, who is a psychiatrist, and who taught at Harvard University, sent me a letter, thanking me for helping him rediscover the infection he once thought he had been cured of. When he asked me for help, I intensified my search for a cure. I worked with some like-minded souls in Texas, and together we developed a method for healing the disease of racism.

There are now more than one hundred Institutes for the Healing of Racism in the United States, the Pacific, Britain and Canada. At these Institutes the infected and wounded come together – in a non-threatening atmosphere – to heal each other. Racial barriers crumble, and people who once harbored ill will for one another embrace as long lost family members – as they were meant to be.

How the Institutes were started, structured and what they have achieved will be described in another chapter of this book. So will a plan on how education can play a role in healing the disease of racism. The plan calls for the integration of the principle of the oneness of humankind in the school curricula, starting with preschoolers and running through the twelfth grade. Why the saturation approach? Because for nearly four hundred years Americans have been exposed to a lie that has been cleverly presented as the truth – that people of

9

color are inferior to whites. A number of public, independent and parochial schools have already adopted the plan.

Both the school plan and the Institutes are based on the principle that the whole determines the behavior of the parts. Most of the prevailing approaches used in trying to solve the racism problem do the opposite. As a consequence, little meaningful progress has been made in overcoming racism in America. Integrating a restaurant in Georgia won't do it; neither will integrating a bus depot in Mississippi or a country club in Pennsylvania. Some progress – true. But what is needed is a different emphasis. More energy should be directed toward dealing with the core of the problem, which remains, for the most part, untouched. This doesn't mean that the battle to break down discriminatory barriers should be discontinued. Bandages and aspirin have their place. But when only the symptoms of a sickness are treated, the disease stands a good chance of worsening. For this reason, this book's purpose is to examine the underlying causes of the disease of racism, and develop ways to cure it.

This book contains several references to weeping and embracing among the wounded and those who cause the wounds. These episodes may be viewed with skepticism by the uninformed. But I write of them unashamedly – to show the powerful impact on the emotions of the realizations brought about by the process of racial healing. These can be shattering, but are necessary for ultimate recovery from the disease.

My hope is that this book will instill in the reader the courage and the fire to address racism, not as a series of isolated social irritants, but as a nationwide disease that is slowly but surely sapping the vitality of a country that has long been considered a refuge for the oppressed and downtrodden. Neglecting to employ such a thrust will, I'm afraid, erode whatever advancements were made in the recent past. There is evidence that this is already happening.

2
Separate but Equal

Most people I have met in different parts of the world – African, Asian or European – believe that as long as humans inhabit our planet racism will exist, mainly because it is natural to distrust the unfamiliar, or dislike what is different from themselves. To prove their point, they refer to history: Not even through the American Civil War, in which six hundred thousand men were killed in a struggle over slavery, was racism eradicated. The Civil Rights Movement, they point out, with all of its fury and high expectations, also failed to solve the core problem.

Their way of keeping the problem from worsening and eventually exploding is to avoid – as much as possible – any involvement with those who appear different and whose ways are different. This notion was actually legalized in 1896 through the U.S. Supreme Court's decision in the Plessy vs. Ferguson case, which called for the establishment of a "separate but equal" social and economic arrangement in a society populated by blacks and whites.

That mandate was only partially carried out. The races remained separate, all right; but blacks never achieved equal social, economic or political status. In fact, most of what they had gained during the Reconstruction period was lost. Jim Crowism, which existed in much of the North as well as the South, replaced slavery. The only difference between the two was that blacks could not be bought or sold. However, in reality, sharecropping, which many Southern blacks were forced to do in order to survive, was a form of slavery. The white landowner, for whom the blacks worked, organized a system that made the blacks dependent upon him for survival. It was ownership without a deed. In the North, blacks, in the main, were subject to de facto segregation in housing and schooling, and were restricted from entering the white-collar work force outside of the black community. The media, meanwhile, reinforced the separate but unequal condition in the United States. This was especially apparent in the movies. Tarzan, who was white and featured as a hero, was seen battling legions of blacks, who were depicted as subhuman savages. I remember, as a child, cheering Tarzan on, wanting him to defeat those strange black creatures. Years later, a black man shared with me and others in a university audience how the Tarzan films affected him when he was a child. I'll never forget the look on that man's face as he shared that painful memory.

In other films, blacks played subservient roles like maids and butlers, or were portrayed as simple-minded men being ordered about by seven- or eight-year-old white children like Shirley Temple. Films that glorified and romanticized racist institutions like the Ku Klux Klan won cinematic awards and wide acclaim by whites in the North and South.

There were no black editors or reporters working for The New York Times or Chicago Tribune. Nor did magazines like Life, Look and the Saturday Evening Post have any. On radio – in the twenties, thirties, forties and early fifties – blacks were relegated to servile roles. Rochester, for example, was comedian Jack Benny's servant. Amos and Andy, who were depicted as two bumbling buffoons in Harlem, were actually played by whites.

In some respects, Jim Crowism was worse than slavery. Between 1890 and 1920, more black men were lynched than were executed by all of the courts in America. The murders were committed with the local and national police making little effort to apprehend the killers. The government's lack of enthusiasm to right the wrongs inflicted on blacks sent a chilling message to the African-American community: *A black's life and property isn't valued as highly as a white's, so don't expect the kind of police protection whites would receive when your rights are violated.*

Blacks, who had a lot of practice coping with bad times, adjusted to the Jim Crow era. This doesn't mean that they accepted the white power structure's view of them – or that they gave up their fight for social justice. Adjustment meant creating the means to survive in an alien culture in order to one day achieve what they felt was due them.

Actually, during the height of the socalled separate but equal period, the Harlem Renaissance came into being, producing poets, novelists, scholars, musical innovators, composers and philosophers like Alain Locke, Roland Hayes, Paul Robeson, Countee Cullen, Langston Hughes and James Weldon Johnson – men who won acclaim in white society, thus dashing some stereotypes held by some members of the establishment regarding blacks' intellectual and creative powers. And certain whites in high places also took notice of the social philosophies of sociologist W.E.B. DuBois, of Booker T. Washington and Marcus Garvey. While all three philosophies differed, more and more whites began to realize that blacks were not content with their lot, that they were plotting ways to change it, and were actually applying pressure on the government to improve its treatment of people of color. In the AfricanAmerican community, the debate over which philosophy would best serve the interests of American blacks energized them, creating a collective determination to improve the black people's social, economic and political condition in their land.

Through Marcus Garvey, who advocated an African-American exodus to Africa, many blacks gained an awareness of their cultural heritage and developed pride in their ancestry. Those who followed Booker T. Washington adopted his gradualist approach to true freedom, which called for maintaining a strong family and learning a good trade that would help keep the family properly fed, sheltered and educated. This was the way, Washington felt, blacks would eventually earn social equality. Many black intellectuals who believed that there was no need to earn what was morally theirs favored DuBois' confrontational approach, which called for the changing of the nation's laws so that all people of color would be truly free, and would be protected by the law if anyone or any group tried to deprive them of their rights and freedoms guaranteed by the U.S. Constitution.

13

Through DuBois' consistent agitating and the help of some wealthy sympathetic whites, the National Association for the Advancement of Colored People was formed – which over the years led the successful legal battle to repeal the Plessy vs. Ferguson ruling.

With the separate but equal approach to resolving the black-white conflict legally dead, the Civil Rights Movement was born. Racial integration became the rage.

But the prize that was sought, and seemed so near, was never attained. This, despite the thousands of protest marches across the nation, despite the fiery rioting in 120 American cities, despite the bombing of black churches and police dogs attacking black children trying to integrate white schools, despite black and white integrationists being killed by the Ku Klux Klan in Mississippi, despite the U.S. Congress passing legislation that guaranteed blacks the right to vote and eliminated all segregated public facilities, despite the assassination of Medgar Evers and Dr. Martin Luther King, recipient of the Nobel Peace Prize for his unstinting and courageous leadership in trying to win equality for America's people of color – despite all of that, and more, the racist social atmosphere throughout the United States remained fundamentally unchanged. Oh, there had been expressions of sympathy for the bombings, lynchings and assassinations; blacks and whites were eating at the same lunch counters and attending the same schools. But the hearts of whites, where the disease of racism festered, hadn't been penetrated. Deep down, most whites still felt that people of color, especially blacks, were inherently inferior. While the Civil Rights Movement was able to create in most whites a greater awareness of the wrongness of racism, it was unable to alter their feelings toward interracial marriage, of living next to a black family, or having a black as one's boss. Conscience-stricken, many whites sought to devise foolproof ways of masking their true feelings toward blacks.

When their overtures of true friendship to whites were rejected, many African-Americans recognized that they really hadn't been accepted as equals. Though the rejections by whites were more tactful than in the past, the pain, in some respects, hurt more than an overseer's whiplash, because it was laced with disappointment – disappointment that, after such a fierce and long struggle, they had been denied what they wanted more than anything else in life – respect as equal citizens in a land they helped to build into what people in other nations believe is the greatest democracy in the world.

I witnessed the rejection manifested by well-meaning white men and women who weren't aware of how they were hurting the very people they wanted to help. I'll never forget the silent sadness and pain expressed by a middle-aged black woman when a white voter registration worker took over her typewriting assignment, because it was felt she wasn't typing fast enough. I have seen white teachers, with loving and caring natures, mentally track a new student if the child is black. Less is automatically expected of the youngster, who intuitively senses what is happening. Because he is powerless to alter the situation, the child's already shaky self-esteem suffers another blow. White corporations hire a few blacks and carefully place them in positions where they'll be easily noticed, thus satisfying the need to be socially progressive, and thereby helping attract lucrative federal government contracts.

This kind of behavior and maneuvering goes on steadily. Though it is a far cry from the Ku Klux Klan's cross burning ritual on a black family's lawn, it's just as disturbing to blacks, who no longer want to experience that kind of treatment, who don't want to be used as a profit-making tool, and who don't want to be pitied by do-gooder white folks any more.

As a consequence, many African-Americans, especially the more educated, are more suspicious of whites than they were thirty or fifty years ago. The young, especially, are alienated, and aren't afraid to show it. The rap songs that move them most are angry expressions against the white man's actions toward blacks in the past and present. They wear baseball caps and T-shirts featuring an "X," for Malcolm X, whose early credo of black separatism they espouse, not the oneness of humankind theme he promoted shortly before he was assassinated.

15

In some cities blacks are building up weapons arsenals, preparing themselves for an armed revolt against the system that they feel is denying them their humanhood. In Milwaukee, a black leader, formerly a member of the City Council, has openly warned the city administration that if his people's lot isn't radically improved in five years, he will personally lead a revolt, which is already being mapped out. Weapons are being collected, and there's no shortage of recruits who are presently being trained for combat.

Even some upper-middle-class blacks living in posh suburbs, who have tried hard to assimilate into the dominant culture, are sending their children to predominantly black colleges. In Amherst, Massachusetts, the daughter of a college professor and a human service organization executive was sent to Hampton University in Virginia instead of Harvard, which had offered her a considerable amount of financial aid. Bill Cosby's son is a graduate of Morehouse College. Cosby also gave Spelman College, a predominantly black, all-women's school, twenty million dollars. In more and more inner-city black neighborhoods, parents want their children to attend all-black schools, staffed only by black teachers and administrators. White teachers, they claim, are insensitive to the needs of black children; and busing black youngsters to predominantly white suburban schools traumatized them. Made to feel out of place, many of them did poorly academically. For the most part, the small cluster of black students were viewed and treated as aliens by their white counterparts and teachers, who were unfamiliar with the African-American culture.

Many liberal whites, meanwhile, are baffled as to why blacks appear to be drawing more and more to themselves, creating their own segregation system. They can't understand why African-Americans, who fought so hard to end racial segregation, no longer want to integrate the Caucasian-dominated society. The most offended whites' reactions are to categorize those blacks who prefer to be with themselves as racists. I have seen that happen time and time again.

During one of my speaking tours I came across a white, blue-eyed and blonde college student who had been so moved by a TV documentary that she wanted to do something for the cause of racial unity. The next day she decided she was going to make friends with some black students who always seemed disconnected from the rest of the campus community. Ignoring warnings from her white friends, she approached a cluster of black students in the college cafeteria. When they rejected her offer of friendship, she went back to her white friends convinced that she should have heeded their advice – and that the black students were, indeed, racists.

When she shared her experience with me, I tried to explain why she had been rebuffed: "Put yourself in their shoes. What if a black student, whom you didn't know, approached you and your friends in the cafeteria, asking to be your friend? Wouldn't you be suspicious? Also, keep this in mind – your overture of friendship was most likely motivated by a desire to help who you perceive as a lowly group of people, who desperately want to be a part of the wonderful white dominant culture – and through the kindness of your heart, you invited them to be a part of that culture. That's how your gesture was interpreted – and no one likes to be pitied. And, besides, while that attitude is benign, it smacks of superiority."

The young woman took to heart what I shared with her, and vowed to work on her attitude toward blacks, an attitude she never knew she had.

An African-American who teaches sociology at a college told me, "Segregation is not the issue; blacks having the right to pursue a segregationist way of life that will serve their best interests is the issue."

"In the past," he went on to say, "the white man established a vicious segregated system and enforced the rules. Now we have created a system, and we enforce the rules."

Interestingly, this system the professor referred to is obviously nothing official; there is no code that has been drafted by the participants' leadership. Born out of necessity, it seems to be a collective need to preserve one's dignity, to conserve one's mental health. In

17

essence, the drive to withdraw from white society is an act of survival.

Isn't it natural to want to pull away from the source of your pain?

Activist Louis Farrakhan knows that. Though most blacks don't belong to Islam, his religion, they are moved by what he has to say, for he articulates clearly and powerfully how they really feel, living in a society that hasn't accepted them as equals. And it isn't only the disenfranchised and poverty-stricken blacks who are moved by Farrakhan: Many of those blacks making six-figure salaries secretly agree with his analysis of the black person's condition in America.

Obviously, regular public pronouncements by highly-respected African-American rights activists like Louis Farrakhan energize the movement of black separatism within the African-American community. Many blacks believe he's telling the truth like no other public figure does – much the way Malcolm X did. When Farrakhan speaks publicly, the auditoriums are filled to capacity, and most in the audience aren't Muslims.

White criticism of Farrakhan only accelerates the drive for separatism. Why? Because it is proof that whites can't understand what the basic problem is. It has been mentioned to them in the past by blacks of various ideological persuasions, employing different voices: the militant's angry rhetoric; the scholar's calm rational explanation; and the preacher's passionate appeal – but it has never really sunk in.

Simply put, whites can't accept the fact that their country is fundamentally racist; and because they have been brought up in that kind of environment, they have been infected. Even the most well-meaning have been infected – like that white college student who tried to befriend blacks.

True, the degree of infection is relative, but, nevertheless, the infection exists. Whites, for the most part, can't see the pollution of racism in America, because they are the pollutant producers. Blacks know this. They know it because they have been trained by their parents on how to best cope in a white man's world, where people of color are not expected to attain real equal status. To train their children well, black parents must have an accurate awareness of the prevailing social climate and make sure the children know what they know. Most of the knowledge, born out of bitter experiences, has been accumulated over the decades and passed on from one genera-tion to another. Without that kind of training, black boys and girls are going to get into trouble. I believe, with all my heart, that there is a correlation today between the high incidence of school dropouts, teenage pregnancies, involvement in drugs and other crimes among black youth, and the fact that black family life is eroding at an alarming rate in America. Some black leaders feel that if their community's young people aren't getting the training that they had received as youngsters, then a way should be found to cut the youth off from the white man's world, which has become a route to defeat and failure for them. But chances of that happening are slim, at best, for a way would have to be found to keep black youth from watching television, reading magazines and newspapers, listening to the radio and going to the movies. Meanwhile, there are elements within the black community who deplore the idea of having to condition children to cope in the white man's world, for resorting to such a practice is felt to be an admission of one's inferiority.

Until whites are able to see what blacks see in terms of the real cause of racism in America, blacks will continue to retreat, as much as they can, from the white-dominant society. Today they are engineering – out of necessity – a separate but equal condition, but without the influence of Jim Crowism, which, they feel, should make life a lot more tolerable than trying to assimilate into a culture that makes them feel like second class citizens. In a way, we have come full circle since the Plessy vs. Ferguson ruling. This time it is the blacks who are demanding separate but equal status.

W hile many liberal whites remain baffled over the African-American drift toward separatism, the great majority of whites quietly applaud it. For to them, it means blacks won't be moving into their neighborhoods; fewer blacks will be bused into their school systems; and their youth won't be fraternizing with black youth, thereby lessening the chances of racial intermarriage. It will be a return to the "good old days."

In my travels I have been exposed to this kind of attitude. And not from racial zealots, but from decent human beings who love their family, love their country, who attend church regularly, and are willing to help a distressed neighbor.

During a flight to the Pacific Northwest one morning, the man sitting next to me and I got into a conversation about America's race problem. In an inquiring mood, I refrained from sharing my views. Instead, I asked questions, and listened.

The man, who ran a successful wholesale hardware business in the Midwest, was an elder in his church, a regular contributor to the Salvation Army, one of the founders of the Rotary Club in his town and a booster of the high school football team.

"We don't have many blacks in our town. Those who live there are long time residents," he said with pride. "You see, our town was part of the Underground Railroad prior to the Civil War. And some of the runaway slaves remained. They have been fine citizens. One of them has a son who is the star of our football team. All sorts of colleges are courting him."

The man again swelled up with pride when he added, "The young man's father has asked me to be his son's advisor."

"Do you employ any of the blacks?" I asked.

"Oh, yes. We have two working for us."

"What do they do at your company?"

"They work in our warehouse. Both are reliable workers."

"What kind of work do the other blacks in your town do?"

"Most of them work at the granary. And one drives a truck for the post office."

Earlier, the man had revealed that a fairly large ball bearing plant had been established in his town and was hiring. When I asked him if he expects more blacks to move into his town because of the plant, he said, "That could be a problem, for most of them would come from other parts of the state where they tend to be more aggressive. I know our police chief is worried."

"Are you worried?"

"Frankly, I am. It's not that I'm prejudiced. I get along fine with the black folks in town. But what scares me is that new ones will most likely alter our way of life, you know, drugs and things like that."

The man paused and looked out the window for a moment, and added, "One good thing, though. Lately, they tend to stick to themselves. They have always had their churches, but now they have their own clubs. And that's the way it should be."

"Why?" I asked.

"That way you avoid a lot of trouble."

Before we landed, he handed me his card and said, "If you happen to be in our area, please give me a ring. I'd like to show you our town, give you a tour of our operation, and if you want to visit the mineral baths – they're world famous – you could spend the night with us. We have lots of room. All of our children are grown and on their own."

While I was impressed by the man's sincerity, I couldn't help but think that there were millions of men and women who, like him, share the same racial views.

The tendency for blacks to reject social integration was the source of joy to a middle-aged woman I met at a reception for a mutual friend of ours. Somehow she learned that I had written a book about racism, and she wanted to share her views on the subject. But before sharing her views, she needed to impress me with her qualifications.

"You know, I have a master's degree in sociology."

"That's good," I said.

"You'd never guess how I've used my education."

"I wouldn't dare."

"I'm into real estate."

"Okay," I said, genuinely interested in what she had to say, "Tell me how you use it to advance your business."

"I can gauge when a neighborhood is going to deteriorate."

"What do you mean by deteriorate?"

"When certain elements somehow find a way of moving into highly-prized neighborhoods."

"Who are these certain elements?" I asked.

"Principally, blacks who are climbing up the corporate ladder."

"Why would they deteriorate a neighborhood?"

"Well, they usually come from big families. Some of their brothers and sisters and cousins come to live with them. And because they are less educated and sophisticated than the owner, they tend to spoil the neighborhood."

The woman then hit me with a barrage of statistics, trying to prove her point that once a black family moves into a neighborhood the value of the houses declines, that it is only a matter of time before the neighborhood becomes predominantly black.

"I watch the trends carefully," she said. "One good thing is happening. Blacks today aren't looking to be real estate pioneers. They don't want to endure the pain any more. And who can blame them? They want to stay with their own kind, which is a blessing for them and us."

3

A Shrinking Planet

While I can understand why there is an impulse among blacks to pull away from the white man's world, it runs counter to humanity's purpose on this planet. The human family is meant to be united. This has become apparent in recent years as science has transcended the natural barriers that have kept peoples apart, and nations – including former enemies – have formed political and economic unions.

Whites who avoid any serious involvement in racial integration have a responsibility to participate in the unifying of the human family. World peace is dependent upon it. As long as one set of humans distrusts another, or feels superior to another group, some form of violence will eventually break out. Finding places to hide is growing more and more difficult in this shrinking planet, whose population is expected to double in fifty years. Learning to live and work together is essential. Despite what some cynics claim, humans didn't come into being to hate one another, to cheat one another, to slaughter one another, or to blow up our planet. True, built into every one of us is the potential to hate, cheat and kill; but we also possess the potential to love, help and heal. The impulse to hate is manifested when the potential to love is neglected. Hatred is a by-product of fear, and fear is an outgrowth of ignorance. It is easier to hate than to love something or someone that seems strange.

The animal in us is aroused, and self-preservation becomes paramount. We strike out blindly, at times violently, at what we perceive is our enemy. Yet, as we attack, there still burns within us a hope that one day there will be peace in the world. I believe this hope is universal; it is a minuscule flicker of light, springing from the bottomless reservoir of love and compassion that is part of all of us, even in those who appear to be the most wicked The more love we generate, the more intense our hope becomes until it evolves into a belief; and the depth of our belief intensifies as our love grows. Today's hater can be tomorrow's lover.

Within both the black and white communities there are men and women who seem to be consumed with hatred of the other race. They dream of and plot ways to eliminate the enemy, and in their minds they can justify what they are contemplating. But their attitude and behavior can change. Today, there are former Ku Klux Klansmen and Nazis who are working tirelessly to break down the barriers of racism. What caused their transformation? With knowledge of what constitutes the reality of man, they overcame certain deep-rooted fears; they discovered and developed the love and compassion that was inherent in them. The potential good within them had been released – and that's a powerful force. Malcolm X was exposed to that force when he went on a pilgrimage to Mecca. Terribly suspicious of whites, he became a forceful advocate of black separatism. When he met some fellow Muslims who were white, his suspicion evaporated. Their generosity and wholehearted love literally overwhelmed him. As a consequence, Malcolm X returned to America committed not only to improving the lot of blacks, but to become a force of unity within the community-at-large.

While we – that is, all of us – possess the capacity to become loving and caring men and women free of suspicion and hatred, our communities, for the most part, reflect a condition that is far from the ideal. People are wallowing in distrust and fear. They are confused as to what – if anything – should be done to overcome racism. Deep down, most of us know that to hate someone because of skin color is wrong. And we are continually reminded of that by television and radio public service spots, newspaper stories, preachers and politicians, teachers and activists. We march in Martin Luther King Junior Day parades, go to race unity picnics, participate in Black History Month celebrations and attend racism workshops given by race-relations experts, yet outbreaks of racism continue to occur on our college campuses, in our elementary schools, in our markets, in our parks, in our theaters, and in the workplace. We know there is a problem, and time and again we are told how bad it is – but our institutional remedies don't really work, despite the outlay of great sums of money to set up special programs. Many of us who clamored for integrated schools through busing see how psychologically harmful they have been for many of those who were supposed to benefit from the system, and are now clamoring for all-black schools with only black teachers. Affirmative Action has in many ways fueled the fire of racism among whites, who accuse the program of fostering reverse racism. In the 1991 Louisiana gubernatorial race, the majority of whites voted, unsuccessfully, for David Duke, the former Nazi and Ku Klux Klan leader; and there were many others who didn't vote for him but who agreed with his racist social and political views.

In a frantic effort to eradicate racism, schools are promoting multicultural education programs that really don't touch the core of the problem. Multiculturalism has become the "in" term, the politically correct panacea to push. In many instances, school systems adopt such programs, not really believing that they will work, but to demonstrate to the public that they are aware of the problem and are doing something about it. It is also hoped that the investment will gag the social agitators, and thus buy some social tranquility.

I met an elderly black man in the South, whose perception of America's race problem provided me with insights I doubt I would have been able to gain on my own. He lit in me a fire that continues to grow.

The man, who only had one arm, approached me after my talk, and thanked me for what I had shared with the audience.

"Normally," he said, "I don't invite a stranger, especially a white man, to my house, but I'd like you to come over as soon as you're through here." The old man grabbed my shoulder and looked me straight in the eye. "There's something I want to give you, something you could use when you speak in the future."

I was intrigued, for whatever it was that was going to make my talks on racism more effective, I wanted. It had to have been past ten p.m., the time I usually prepare for bed. But I had to go with that man, for in recent years I have had some strange experiences that have produced insights into the race problem, insights that have helped me gain a deeper understanding of the causes of racism, thus aiding me in my struggle to find solutions. Some might call those experiences a clear case of serendipity. I feel there is a more specific explanation: They have been answers to prayer.

The old man assured my host and hostess that he would take good care of me and deliver me to their place in one piece. I sensed that they were reluctant to let me go, because they didn't know the man, and rarely ventured into the black neighborhood, especially at night.

He lived alone in a one-story, white-frame bungalow with a porch, featuring a wooden swing that I suspect he used more and more as he reflected on his past and what might lie in store for his countrymen in the near future. Obviously, I had no evidence how he used the swing, if he used it at all. It just struck me that the slightly stooped, white-haired gentleman was a deep thinker.

Inside the house, I noticed a picture of him as a soldier in World War II. There was also a picture of him with a woman who must have been his wife, and three of their children. She seemed fairly young, and the boys about eight, six and four. I surmised that he was a widower, or divorced, and that his children were grown and gone. There was no other evidence in the house of someone else living there.

The old man was seated in a brown leather club chair, facing a black-and-white television set.

He sighed and said, "You're probably wondering what it is I want to tell you."

"Yes, I am."

"I'll get right to the point," he said. "Most white folks don't like to beat around the bush like us black folks."

"I guess I fall into that category," I said. "I don't like to waste words – or time."

"But Nathan, beating around the bush is not always a waste of words or time. In many instances it is a means of smoothing the way to the other person's mind and heart."

"I never thought of that," I said. "I guess it makes for better communication."

"Right," he said.

While I understood his message, it didn't alter my desire to know immediately what he wanted to tell me. My impatience wasn't directed at the old man; it stemmed from my need to know what he had in mind. I sensed that whatever he was going to tell me would be helpful.

"Nathan, I have heard a lot of speeches about human rights, about civil rights, in my day, but I never heard anyone, especially a white guy, say what you said tonight. It moved me."

"Thank you," I said, not knowing what else to say, and trying hard to hide my embarrassment.

"It wasn't the intellectual content that was so spectacular."

"Oh," I said, reeling a bit from the blow to my ego.

"It is your honesty and sincerity that moved me, and I'm sure other blacks were moved, as well as some whites.

"You told the truth, that racism is a disease, that you were infected, and the way you explained your struggle to heal yourself moved me so much that the barrier of self-defense that I had built during the years was penetrated. I literally wanted to reach out and hug you. That's right, hug you, a white man, something I was sure I would never do in my lifetime. Not after what I've been through.

"Going to inferior segregated schools, going off to war to fight an enemy of democracy and getting my arm blown off at the Battle of the Bulge, and, when I came home wearing my uniform and Purple Heart ribbon, being told by a restaurant manager that I had to go to the back door if I wanted a hamburger. I wanted to kill the son-of-a-bitch."

The old man glanced at the picture of his family, and said, "They killed my wife and three sons, by setting fire to our home when I was gone one week."

Stunned, I asked, "But why would they do such a thing?"

"To set an example as to what would happen to other blacks who dared to change the racial condition in town. You see, I was viewed as an agitator, because I helped to form a branch of the NAACP and demanded better schooling for the black kids."

"Didn't the police do anything?" I asked.

"Hell, no! I suspect some of them were part of the torching party. No, the fire was officially called an accident, but you can be sure that everyone in town – black and white – got the message."

"What did you do after the fire?"

"I went north – to Boston."

"Was it any better?" I asked.

"Not really. I spent twenty years there, working for a while as a presser for a Jewish immigrant who operated a dry cleaning store in Dorchester, which was a Jewish section in those days. Through a night school program, I earned a high school equivalency certificate and an associate's degree from a community college. And that helped me get a job as a counselor for at-risk youth in Dorchester, which had turned black and as segregated – not lawfully, mind you – as it was in the South thirty years ago."

"How come you returned to the South?" I asked.

"Hell, I thought I never would when I left here," he laughed. "When I heard from my brother that things had changed down here, I came down to check it out. He was right. In many ways it was more comfortable, and a lot safer than Boston.

"There are still places where a black person can't go at night without risking being assaulted by a white gang. I remember the day when a white man in South Boston tried to skewer a black business-man with the staff of an American flag. I got the message.

"And even many of the people who classify themselves as liberals were hard to take. Their condescending attitude drove me up the wall. After a while I didn't want anything to do with them. I know they meant well, but their racism was so apparent."

"How?" I asked, wanting to know how I could avoid doing the same thing.

"Whenever I was with them, they would usually raise the subject of civil rights, or mention something wonderful a black person had recently done, or explain why they thought Oprah Winfrey was so much better as a TV talk show host than Phil Donahue. I was rarely treated as just another human being who had other interests. I was their black friend – never their friend."

What he had shared with me was familiar, because I had often done the same thing with black people I thought I was getting close to – and was always puzzled as to why I would never see them again. Curious, I asked him if he had ever confronted his well-meaning tormentors.

"Twice," he said.

"And what happened?"

"Both were offended. One of them cried. The other became angry. Both tried to explain all the things they had done for the civil rights cause and the favors they had done for black folks, the money they had contributed to the NAACP and the Negro College Fund. Because of their reaction, I vowed never to do it again."

"Denial!" I said.

"Yes, denial. It's the biggest barrier to overcoming racism."

"Why?" I asked.

"Because it is the people with the greatest power to change things who suffer from it the most. As long as they don't recognize their infection they'll continue to place Band-Aids on areas where surgery is needed. The cancer will spread."

The old man ran his hand over his hair, then added, "And these people think they're doing good – they really do. Like the year I left Massachusetts – 1989. The Massachusetts Board of Regents for Higher Education voted to prohibit racism in the state's colleges."

The old man threw his head back and laughed, not because he thought what he had just said was funny, but because of the absurdity of the idea.

"That's like proclaiming an end to cancer without providing a cure," he said.

Pausing a moment, he leaned toward me and looked at me as a caring mentor looks at his student. "Now – what you're doing is part of the cure."

"Me?" I asked, stunned.

"Yes – you!" he said, pointing at me.

"I'm not quite sure what you mean," I said.

"You're telling the truth. That's the cure – the truth. Now, it isn't that you're saying something new. Black folks have known what you're talking about for a long time, and those of us who dared to say what you're saying in public were never really heard.

"The people we tried hard to reach called us militants, radicals, even subversives. Others said we weren't grateful for all the wonderful things the government and charities were doing for us.

"But when a person like yourself – a white man – says what we know is the truth, other whites usually listen to him, especially if he's sincere and isn't an opportunist trying to make a name for himself – or a quick buck.

"You have to keep doing what you're doing, because you're like a mirror that allows them to see their infection."

"How does that work?" I asked.

"When you tell how you discovered your racist feelings, and how you still struggle with those feelings, they are able to identify with what you are undergoing, and they are encouraged to do the same thing. And that will set off a process of healing that'll snowball.

"Also – part of telling the truth is telling folks how racism came into being in America. Everyone needs to deal with the fact – and I know this may be hard to take – that our country is fundamentally racist. We need to know how it got that way. Without that knowledge, it would be very difficult to liberate ourselves from a falsehood, manufactured by misguided men in the past into what has been accepted as the truth by all Americans for nearly three hundred years."

"You mean blacks bought into it?"

"Absolutely. On the surface we may deny it, but deep down it has been embraced. Why do you think there is so much black-on-black violence? Self-hatred. It was perfectly natural that that would happen when you consider that generation after generation of blacks and whites were exposed to white clergymen, politicians, judges, philosophers and scientists preaching white superiority and black inferiority."

"Brainwashing!" I said.

"You can call it that. But the only cure is the truth – the truth encouraged and fostered by the nation's leadership."

"But for that to happen, a collective admission is required that our nation is fundamentally racist, that the Founding Fathers were racist, that we have lived a lie all of these years. I'm afraid that for that to happen a miracle is required," I said.

"Not necessarily. I know it is a lot to ask for. But it has to be done. All that's necessary is a vision and conviction, and to make a beginning. And you and people like you have already started. The idea is not to stop. Remember, an acorn is a potential forest. That's why it is important that you and your colleagues continue what you are doing, even accelerate what you're doing. We need to know the truth. I really believe that it is the truth that will eventually make Americans free."

While, at the time, I understood what the old man had told me, I wasn't sure about my role in his vision of what's needed to heal the disease and wound of racism in America. After all – who am I, I thought. Just a teacher in an obscure New England college, who has written a few books that most people have never heard of; who has produced a few documentaries that few people have seen. I'm no historian or sociologist, no member of a highly-respected human rights commission, no advisor to a governor, mayor or community relations director. True – I feel strongly about racism, but so do many others who are eminently more qualified to speak about the problem and who appear regularly on nationwide television. I've never been invited to such shows. Nor have I spoken to mass audiences. All I'd done was write a book in which I expose an aspect of myself that, at one time, I never knew was within me. Strange – that though I have had doubts about my ability to carry out what the old man urged me to do, I have kept doing it for more than three years.

Why do I do it? I think the old man knew what would happen if I kept doing what he had urged me to do. I would eventually see that some people who hear me would gain a new awareness of themselves, they would find a way to heal an infection they never knew they had. And some of the wounded would find hope.

The letters and phone calls from people whose attitudes have changed because they have read *To Be One*, or have heard me share what the old man asked that I share, have spurred me on. As for my doubts? They began to fade as more and more people benefited from the message.

One day, while I was in Texas, my doubts vanished. It was a profound experience – and I suspect the more than one hundred men and women attending the race unity conference were also moved by what they saw.

At one session I was seated next to an African-American man from New Mexico with white hair and a closely-cropped beard. When I introduced myself, he asked, "Are you the one who wrote the book?"

I knew he was referring to *To Be One*, and answered, "Yes."

Tears welled up in his eyes, and for a moment he didn't say anything. But soon his reserve broke down, and he began to weep. The only thing I could do was embrace him. We stayed locked in each other's arms for quite a while, oblivious to everything around us. I could feel his body heaving as he sobbed. The buzz in the ballroom stopped.

I cried, too. The tears we shed didn't stem from a sense of sadness. We were like two brothers finally united after living in different worlds most of our lives. But we weren't only together, we had found freedom. We now knew what had kept us apart, and we were free to talk about it. We no longer had to pretend; there were no barriers to contend with.

As we held onto each other, we could sense things about one another without uttering a word. He allowed me to see the black man's wound, caused by centuries of oppression; he was shedding the pain he felt the day he was born. He was now free to find his true self; to be what a human being is meant to be. And he felt confident that the person he was embracing would never try to keep him from finding his true self, and making the most of his potentialities.

I'm sure he sensed from me an openness, a sincere reaching out that wasn't apparent to others or to myself before the poison of racism started to drain from my heart. He also sensed a genuine love for him, based on the principle I had always endorsed, but never understood until I seriously began my struggle to heal the infection within me – and that was the oneness of humankind.

At that moment, I couldn't help but feel what an important role my conviction had played in my quest to be free of racism. I was sure that the man in my arms felt the same way.

4
All One Family

I doubt if I'll ever forget that bonding experience at the race unity conference in Texas – nor will my partner that day; and I suspect those who witnessed it will remember it for a long time as well. It was more than a stimulant to continue the fight for racial equality. To me it symbolized the condition the human family was meant to attain and preserve – and that is unity.

By unity I don't mean a truce between nations, a toleration between peoples, a geopolitical coexistence scheme, a backyard acquaintanceship with a neighbor. Nothing as fragile as that. What I mean is a unity springing from an understanding of the principle of the oneness of humankind. Because the black man and I understood oneness, we embraced without reservation. It was a genuine urge to reach out to each other. We had no doubts about our belonging to the family of man – and our need to love one another. Without an understanding and internalization of that aspect of reality, true unity is impossible. Good intentions are not enough. Even many religious groups make attempts at unity, and fail. At devotional services and fellowship gatherings they create a caring face while riddled with serious doubts about others, especially those with different colored skin. An air of unspoken insecurity dominates the meeting. They act nicely toward each other at the meeting, but rarely see one another outside of the religious center.

Failure at unity usually results when people don't understand how the internalization of oneness leads to unity. Though both stem from the same reality, oneness is a principle, a fundamental truth, and unity is a process. Coming from the same source, the human family has always been one, but never unified – which, believe it or not, is its destiny. In a way, oneness is like a seed, with the mechanics of unity inherent in it. Under the right conditions, growth, which is a process, takes place; and the seed is on its way to fulfilling its destiny. In the human condition, when a person understands, internalizes and puts into practice the principle of the oneness of humankind, the inherent mechanism of unity is activated within him. He develops a will to bring people together – and does it.

What does this discourse on oneness and unity have to do with racism? A lot. Racism is a natural outgrowth of a multicultural society that's ignorant of the principle of the oneness of humankind. Erroneous assumptions are made about certain people based on superficial differences, causing barriers to arise between ethnic groups. In reality, racism is an aberration of nature. Should that same society overcome its ignorance of oneness, it would no longer be plagued by racism. The impulse for unity will be too great.

Now, I wasn't born with an understanding of oneness. In fact, I spent most of my life, like most of my friends, relatives and teachers, oblivious to the principle of the oneness of humankind and the interconnectedness of all that is. I was a captive of what my senses registered, and what I was told by teachers who took a mechanistic view of life and the universe. Separation seemed so obvious, I thought. Why bother to question it? Yet, signs of oneness were all around me. In a way, I was like the fish who wondered where the ocean was.

My understanding of oneness was gained through study of the Bahá'í teachings. But it wasn't something I grasped immediately. It took years before I understood that the millions of species making up life, including humanity, are fluctuating aspects or focal points of a living organism called Earth that functions as a dynamic, micro-scopic cell in a continuously changing boundless body called the universe – which, incidentally, means "one song." When you break down the word universe, you discover that *uni* means one and *verse* means song. And we – all of the nearly six billion humans on Earth

35

– comprise some of the notes of one song.

All that exists is interrelated. Take, for example, eating, drinking and breathing: In reality, we eat, drink and breathe the Earth – and also the sun and our galaxy and the universe. For are not bread and meat and rain part of the Earth? And is not the Earth part of the sun? And the sun part of our galaxy, and all of them part of the universe? Buddhist philosopher Thich Nhat Hanh has a wonderful way of explaining interrelatedness or oneness. He uses a piece of paper as an example. The paper-making process, he points out, begins with clouds. For the rain, which comes from clouds, produces and maintains the tree, from which the paper is made. Without the logger and the truck driver the tree wouldn't be hauled to the mill where it is processed. Of course, the interrelatedness chain in making a piece of paper can be extended beyond the parents of the logger and truck driver. But there's no need to go on, for I think you get the point.

Since humanity is a part of the universe, it has to be interconnected, despite what some human beings with distorted views of reality proclaim. The millions of known species on Earth are aspects of a single reality. Humans are part of a species we call Homo sapiens. While all species have different capacities and functions, they all share some similar qualities, which makes for universal linkage. For example, the power of attraction, which keeps the atoms of a rock together, exists in humans; the plant, like the rock, possesses the power of attraction, plus the powers of growth and reproduction, which are evident in man; the animal contains the qualities of the rock and plant as well as sensory powers and consciousness, which we also possess.

What distinguishes humans from the animal is the power of ideation, the ability to be conscious of our consciousness, and a spiritual dimension. Now, Homo sapiens is, in reality, one family, regardless of skin color, geographical location, facial features and hair texture.

Many highly respected thinkers recognize the reality of oneness, including paleontologist Richard Leakey, who wrote more than a decade ago:

"We are one species, one people. Every individual on this earth is a member of Homo sapiens sapiens, and the geographical variations we see among peoples are simply biological nuances on the basic theme. The human capacity for culture permits its elaboration in widely different and colorful ways. The often very deep differences between those cultures should not be seen as divisions between people. Instead, cultures should be interpreted for what they really are: the ultimate declaration of belonging to the human species."

I know it is difficult for some people to accept the idea that everyone in the world is related. But that's a fact.

In his book, *The Seven Mysteries of Life*, noted science writer Guy Murchie explains what makes the family of man a reality:

"... no human being (of any race) can be less closely related to any other human than approximately fiftieth cousin, and most of us (no matter what color our neighbors) are a lot closer. Indeed this low magnitude for the lineal compass of mankind is accepted by the leading geneticists I have consulted (from J.B.S. Haldane to Theodius Dobzhansky to Sir Julian Huxley), and it means simply that the family trees of all of us, of whatever origin or trait, must meet and merge into one genetic tree of all humanity by the time they have spread into our ancestries for about fifty generations. This is not a particularly abstruse fact, for simple arithmetic demonstrates that, if we double the number of our ancestors for each generation as we reckon backward (consistently multiplying them by two: 2 parents, 4 grandparents, 8 great-grandparents, 16 great, great grandparents, etc.), our personal pedigree would cover mankind before the thirtieth generation. Mathematics is quite explosive in that regard, you see, for the thirtieth power of two (1,073,741,824) turns out to be much larger than was the earth's population thirty generations ago – that is, in the thirteenth century if we assume 25 years to a generation."

Yes, the Inuit of Northern Alaska, the Hasidic Jew in Jerusalem, the Watusi tribesman of Central Africa, the Lakota Indian of South Dakota, the Chinese, the Japanese, the Mexican and the white Anglo-Saxon Protestant of Greenwich, Connecticut, are our cousins.

The birth of a child to an interracial couple is a sign of belonging to the human family, since the mother and father must be of the same species in order to reproduce. I mention this because there are people who believe that Africans, Europeans, American Indians, Latinos and Asians are different species, just as dogs, rats and cats are different species. Obviously, this warped notion is disproved every time an interracial couple produces a child. I've never heard of a gorilla and a human producing offspring.

As for those who believe that interracial marriages produce inferior children, James King, professor of microbiology at New York University School of Medicine, debunks that myth: "Several extensive studies of hybrid populations have been made and they show no evidence for reduction in viability, fertility, or functional efficiency in the first, second, or later generations of hybrids between unlike human populations. These studies include one on Dutch-Hottentot hybrids in South Africa made more than 60 years ago, one made in the 1920s on the descendants of the mutineers of the Bounty, and the elaborate study of the 179,000 babies of mixed Caucasian-Oriental-Polynesian descent born in Hawaii between 1948 and 1958."

Human blood is another proof that people everywhere, regardless of skin color, hair texture and geographical location, belong to the same species, the same family. Four blood types (A, B, AB, and O) are found in all human ethnic groups. No other species' blood is going to save the life of a human. On the other hand, a sickly Englishman with Type O blood can receive a transfusion from a Ghanaian with Type O blood, with successful results.

Now, there are some people who believe that whites are closest to the chimpanzee, because they share some similar physical traits like straight hair, thin lips, light skin (check out a totally shaved chimp) and fairly flat bottoms.

Professor King debunks that myth as well: ".... when the measurements of protein differences within the human species are compared with those between ape and human, the latter are from 25 to 60 times as great as any difference between two human populations, and neither Caucasians, black Africans, nor Japanese are any nearer to the chimpanzee than either of the others."

Not only are all the people living in Africa, Asia, Europe, the Pacific Islands, Latin and North America members of the same family, they are linked by an invisible chain. How? Through breathing. To appreciate this aspect of reality, it is important to know that the atom is the fundamental building block in the substance we call physical life. Without atoms there would be no molecules; without molecules there would be no cells, without cells there would be no tissue; without tissues there would be no organs; and without organs we wouldn't exist.

According to endocrinologist Deepak Chopra, every time we inhale we take in trillions of atoms, once part of others, that end up as part of us – even our brain cells, heart cells, and our DNA; and, with each breath, we exhale trillions of atoms that actually are bits and pieces of our tissues and organs, exchanging them with everyone else on our planet.

Yes, the Ku Klux Klansman may possess atoms that were once a part of a black man from Harlem or Mississippi, and vice versa.

So you can see that the idea of a "pure" race has always been a groundless assumption – pure fantasy.

Though we are all at least fiftieth cousins, everyone is different. There are no two humans that are exactly alike. We all have our own individuality. For example, no two people have the exact same fingerprints.

Now, the fact that there are differences between us doesn't conflict with the principle of oneness. God loves variety as well as unity. As a result, the universe operates on the principle of unity and diversity. It is as real as the law of gravity, and is manifested in every level of life, even among look-alikes. A sandy beach, for example, may appear from the boardwalk as a gray- or beige-colored mass. When we scoop up a handful of sand and examine each grain, however, we find that each one has its own particular size and shape. Upon close scrutiny, we discover that in a bed of red roses some flowers have more petals, are shorter or taller and are in different stages of maturity. The same is true among animals, not only in physique but in temperament as well. Though all four of my children are different, they are linked through their roots. Very much like a tree. None of a tree's branches, twigs, leaves and fruits are exactly alike, yet they are part of a whole, tied to one set of roots.

"The diversity of the human family," said Abdu'l Bahá, "should be the cause of love and harmony; as it is in music where many different notes blend together in the making of a perfect chord."

There are people on our planet who aren't familiar with the scientific data that proves that all humans are related. In fact, they may have never heard of the term, "the oneness of humankind" – yet they understand it and practice it without reservation.

My son Dale, who now lives in Papua New Guinea, has met some of these people. While visiting his in-laws in the Solomon Islands, Dale followed an intuitive flash to check out the job market in nearby Papua New Guinea. He's a television director and writer and film maker.

The same day he arrived in Port Moresby he was offered a job by the leading advertising agency in the Papua New Guinea capital. Later that day, he called on the local Bahá'ís. A number of them invited him to visit a Bahá'í village about fifty miles from Port Moresby. Curious, he accepted.

Night had fallen when the pickup truck they were in stopped at the edge of a forest. The next leg of the journey would be by foot. Dale followed his friends through the dense woods, wondering – at times – what was in store for him.

When they emerged from the forest, Dale found himself in a clearing, with a star-studded sky and full moon above. Ahead was a river. One of his new friends went to the edge of the river, cupped his mouth with his hands and called out a Bahá'í greeting several times: "Alláh'u'Abhá!" ("God the most glorious!") In a matter of seconds lights started to pop on across the river, and hundreds of voices responded with Alláh'u'Abhá. Soon the chant blossomed into song which resounded through the area. In a matter of minutes, canoes came to fetch Dale and his party.

When they arrived at the village, the people were still singing. Some of them approached Dale and his friends with flowers and fruit. Every face he looked at – young and old, male or female – was graced by a smile. Instinctively, he knew that the smiles sprang from pure love. Never before had Dale been embraced by that kind of love. Moved, he began to weep. "For the first time in my life," he said to himself, "I feel spiritually alive."

An elderly man, who noticed that Dale was crying, embraced him and whispered into his ear, "You are my son. You are my son." Dale knew that the elderly man believed what he had said; that he had accepted as a member of his family a young white man who lived halfway around the world in a place he had never heard of before, and a culture he was completely unfamiliar with.

In a few minutes, Dale felt closer to the elderly man and the other villagers than most of the people he had known for a long time back home. There were no psychological barriers between him and the people of a village that has yet to appear on a map. Dale felt that his heart had blended with the hearts of everyone in the village. The unity he experienced was the result of everyone there completely accepting him and his party as members of their family. Their love was so great that Dale couldn't do anything but reciprocate in kind. It was a feeling he'll never forget, for it allowed him to discover an aspect of reality he had read about in Bahá'í books, but never thought he would ever experience.

Each man, one white, one black, from different worlds, saw an aspect of himself in the other's eyes. In this case, it was their common religion that allowed them to see past the physical barriers, past the worldly affectations, to the true soul of the other. Surely, I thought, as Dale conveyed his story to me, there must be some vehicle, some tool for understanding, that we could develop in the United States that would do the same.

41

5
Among the Blind

The principle of the oneness of humankind had become real to me. Now that I understood it, and wanted to live it, it seemed so obvious. I wondered why the great majority of people in the world weren't aware of it.

I didn't have to ponder that question long. Prejudice was blinding people from recognizing what was as natural as the air we breath.

What is prejudice? An emotional commitment to ignorance. Because we fear what we don't know, we don't want to have anything to do with what we fear.

Take, for example, a person who has never seen a frog before. During a walk in the woods, he notices a frog perched on a rock. He is immediately repulsed by the appearance of the creature, and doesn't want anything to do with frogs. But one day the man learns of the frog's contribution to the planet's ecosystem, and his view of the frog changes; he's glad that there are frogs, and becomes their advocate. Through knowledge the man overcomes his emotional commitment to ignorance toward frogs.

On a more personal note: I had a deep-rooted prejudice toward Christians. As a child and a youth I lived in a Jewish ghetto in the South Bronx. It was a tough place. Swiping stuff from Woolworth's five-and-ten cents store was considered a heroic deed. So was bashing a Christian. It didn't matter that I didn't know anything about Christianity. In fact, I didn't want to know. I would become enraged at the sight of a cross. My friends and I were convinced that Christianity was an evil force, for we were aware of the Christian-instigated persecution of Jews that lasted for nearly two thousand years. We knew that Nazi Germany was a Christian country, and we knew what it was like to be called "Christ killer!" and what it was like to be despised.

This became clear when I was about eight years old during a motor trip to Boston. Many of my relatives lived there. In those days it took eight hours – if you were lucky – to get from New York to Boston. There were no expressways linking the cities. When my father got lost in a rural area of northern Connecticut, he drove to a general store, hoping someone there would give us good directions. He knew that, away from New York City, he would be dealing with someone he considered was a real American. To him, a real American was blond, blue-eyed and spoke impeccable English. He wanted so badly to be considered a real American; maybe that's why he tried hard to mask his thick Russian accent and fractured use of his adopted language. He took me by the hand and said, "Let's go."

The proprietor of the store was a real American. Trying to talk like a Yankee, and failing miserably at it, my father asked for directions to Boston. I'll never forget the look of disdain on the proprietor's face as he listened to my father struggling to be understood and accepted. That look made my blood boil. The man was stripping my father of his dignity – and I could sense that my father knew what was happening. I wanted to choke the "real American" behind the counter.

My hatred of Christians was so intense that I found pleasure in beating up Christian guys. It was a thrill, because every time my fist landed on the kid's face, I felt I was avenging what his people had done to my people.

Because of that experience, I can understand what drives a black or Latino youth today to strike out blindly, at times violently, against what he feels is his traditional persecutor. While I no longer condone that kind of behavior, I know what it feels like to want to strike out. It is real, born out of rage and frustration and a desire for some sort of justice. It is a primal cry for freedom.

I overcame my prejudice toward Christians after becoming a Bahá'í. I didn't always believe there was a difference between prejudice and racism. I would often use the two terms interchangeably. But now I am aware of the difference, having studied how racism came into being in America.

Racism has to do with power. It is institutionalized race prejudice. It comes into being when a government creates or sanctions a prevailing prejudice toward a particular people in order to dominate them so they can be used to increase the fortunes of the powerful and those in control.

Certainly, Nazi Germany was a racist country; and the Republic of South Africa falls into that category. But somehow we find it difficult to categorize the United States of America, one of the world's greatest democracies, as a racist nation. I know I had difficulty accepting that reality, for I love my country. There's a lot good about it.

People all over the world want to emigrate to America, to partake of its freedoms and opportunities to grow, not only materially, but intellectually and spiritually. Yet, considering how my country was founded and developed, I can no longer deny the fact that it is a racist state. I know there are people of good will who are ashamed of what was done by the Founding Fathers in terms of condoning slavery, and state that they shouldn't be blamed for what took place in the past, since they champion the causes of the downtrodden and oppressed in their midst. But it isn't a matter of casting blame; it's a matter of accepting the truth, of understanding the nation's actual social condition.

What was done in the past can't be ignored in the development of a society, no more than an adult can ignore his childhood as a factor in shaping his attitudes and behavior. In order to correct bad behavior, knowledge of its cause is necessary. We can't wish racism away. For it's not like a simple prejudice. The disease of racism that afflicts so many of us is reinforced almost every day when we watch television, read a newspaper, are on the job or attend classes.

Taking vows to be tolerant of one another won't remove the racism that is part of the DNA of the United States of America.

Despite the efforts of well-meaning citizens, manifestations of racism continually arise which usually aren't apparent to them. In a way, it is like the person who lives in Los Angeles and doesn't know what smog is until he goes somewhere else and breathes clean air. Racism occurs every day in every part of America. An example is the use, in what is believed to be a progressive school, of a U.S. history textbook that devotes 350 pages to the exploits of white people, and thirty pages to the contributions of people of color. It doesn't help that the book includes pictures of Dr. Martin Luther King, Jr. and Chief Sitting Bull. While the students – white, brown, yellow and black – don't protest, they can count, and they can reason: If 350 pages are devoted to whites, then the whites must be more important – and superior. As for the teachers, they usually don't challenge the structure of the textbook, for they don't see anything wrong. After all, they reason, favorable mention is made of people of color.

The existence of black and white neighborhoods is usually the result of the policies of banks and real estate establishments which have the effect of keeping the races apart. The theory behind this practice is that when "inferiors" are allowed to live among whites, the neighborhood's economic and social value declines.

Movies that many whites believe promote racial harmony actually expose the film makers' unconscious racism involving blacks, and thereby inadvertently reinforce existing racist attitudes in the audience. Many whites can't understand why many blacks abhor a film like *Guess Who's Coming to Dinner?*, which was hailed by critics as socially daring, and way ahead of its time. Many African-Americans don't like it because it demonstrates that a black person can only attain acceptance in a white-dominated society if he successfully adopts its values and standards, and abandons the cultural values he was brought up with – which the establishment deems inferior.

In other words, if he acts and thinks like a successful white person, his brown- or tan-colored skin becomes less of a barrier, and he stands a better chance of succeeding in America. The whites, meanwhile, who shed tears of joy while watching the young black world-renowned scientist being accepted by an upper-class white family, are making a racist statement. What they are saying, without realizing it, is that white is superior and black is inferior. What is

45

valued is the white world the protagonist steps into, not the black world he came from. In fact, the latter is ignored.

Even the Academy Award-winning film *Driving Miss Daisy* had little appeal among blacks. For, again, blacks are portrayed as second-class citizens. Despite exhibiting strong character traits, the blacks in the film don't have an equal relationship with the whites. It is apparent who holds the real social power.

In the minds of most whites, and many people of color, is an image of the "All-American Boy." It isn't of a black, an American Indian, a Latino or an Asian. It is of a white Anglo-Saxon Protestant – the kind of person that was continually portrayed as a hero by the media.

I remember that when I was growing up, the leading comic book heroes were all white: Captain America, Superman, Captain Marvel, The Human Torch and Batman. On radio, Jack Armstrong, who was portrayed as a typical white Anglo-Saxon Protestant, was actually called the "All-American Boy" by the announcer who introduced each episode. And there was the Henry Aldrich series, which was about the hometown adventures of an idyllic American family – which was white. All of the heroes of thrillers like "The Green Hornet" and "The Lone Ranger" were white, and their companions, who functioned more like servants, were people of color. In fact, Tonto, the name of the Lone Ranger's trailmate, means "dumb one" in Spanish. Until the mid-1970s, television programming followed the same pattern.

True, today, after a considerable amount of protesting by civil rights political action groups and legal action, more people of color are appearing on TV, but seldom as a white's boss. In commercials a black is rarely, if ever, shown as a physician promoting a medicine, or a pilot extolling the virtues of his airline. Why? Because the viewers, including many people of color, still believe that whites are smarter, more trustworthy, more responsible. And it doesn't matter that the U.S. secretary of health and human services is an African-American. The people who produce national TV commercials continually probe, through scientific forms of measurement, the mind-sets of their audiences. Consequently, they're aware of the prevailing attitudes, and won't produce a commercial that would scare the prospective buyers of a product they're promoting.

Of course, there are those social observers who point to the fact that the picture of basketball star Michael Jordan, who is black, has graced the box of Wheaties, the "Breakfast of Champions." While that kind of progress can't be discounted, does the white mind truly accept Michael Jordan as an equal, or is he viewed as an outstanding member of a species that has more animal-like traits like agility, speed and leaping ability than whites? From conversations I have had with many whites in different parts of the country I feel they either believe that special species theory, or have a sneaking suspicion it is true. Of course, revealing that belief or suspicion in public isn't done these days, for that would be politically incorrect. Nevertheless, the belief and suspicion exists among many whites.

African-Americans, who have become well known in their respective fields, know that they haven't reached the same realm of respectability as their white counterparts when they are introduced as a black artist, a black poet or a black writer. The late poet Robert Hayden – a friend of mine – used to bristle every time he was called a black poet. It wasn't that he was trying to hide the fact that he was black. To him that kind of introduction was a sign that somehow he wasn't quite good enough to be lumped together with a Robert Penn Warren, a T.S. Eliot or an Allen Ginsberg, who were never called white poets. And it didn't matter that Hayden served two successive terms as poet-in-residence at the Library of Congress, an honor equivalent to being the nation's poet laureate.

That kind of psychological segregation exists because, deep down, whites who make those kinds of introductions from the platform or in print feel blacks are inferior to whites. When evaluating black and white performance in schools, the teacher automatically creates in her mind separate categories with different criteria as to what is outstanding. The black child isn't supposed to do as well as the white child. It is a known fact that college admission offices have separate criteria for evaluating white and black applicants.

Racism is so deep-rooted in America, so pervasive, so convoluted, that the act of a college making special allowances for black youths reinforces the feeling that blacks are inferior to whites.

The fact that African-American students receive less training to take college admission standardized tests, and that the tests' content is usually culturally biased, has little effect on that feeling. This is one of the reasons why more and more black youths prefer going to colleges that cater primarily to African-American students. It isn't because they think the academic demands will be less, it is because they want to either rid themselves of the "inferiority" stigma, or avoid being tagged with it.

Getting rid of that stigma is difficult, but ridding oneself of being ashamed of being black is more complicated and painful. I met a couple of students at Phillips Exeter Academy, an elite prep school in New England, who were struggling with the reality of being black. After I spoke to the student body, a reception was held for me. In the small group were two young black women who wanted to share their wounds with me. Evidently, something I had said in the auditorium had inspired them to come forth. The older one spoke for both of them:

"There is something I want to say that I have never said to any adult – including my parents."

"And what is that?"

It was obvious that it was difficult for her to reveal what she wanted me to know. Because she felt I could help her, she persisted: "I wish I weren't black."

"Why?" I asked.

"Because I don't think I'm as good as a white person."

"What makes you think that way?"

"I don't know."

When she looked away from me, I sensed that she did know, but found it too painful to share. For me to continue to probe in that setting, I thought, would be too risky for her and her friend. Besides, how could I help them? I had no magical cure. What was needed was the kind of environment that the Institute for the Healing of Racism provides.

Though I answered questions from others in the group, and described the aims of the Institute and urged them to form one at the school, what I remember most about that experience was the pain of the two young black women, both obviously from affluent families, yet emotionally deprived, unable to cope with a reality they wish was only a bad dream. They are victims of racism. But they aren't alone: The whole country is affected by it in one way or another. The particularly virulent form of racism that was brought to North America by Europeans nearly four hundred years ago exists today, even in the hearts of those who claim to be free of it.

The wound that afflicts the black person also afflicts the child of a black and white union. Unlike in South Africa, where there are several well recognized ethnic distinctions, in America there's no special racial category – no place of belonging – for a person of mixed racial stock. A person whose parents were black and white usually fails in an attempt to create a separate identity after experiencing resistance and, at times, hostility from both blacks and whites. Frustrated and wanting to belong somewhere, the individual winds up thinking of himself or herself as black. It is important to note that this decision, which is based on convenience rather than conviction, doesn't dissipate the individual's inner torments and conflicts.

Michelle Renwick-Carrera, a teacher, and a graduate of Smith College in Northampton, Massachusetts, where she lives, has herself experienced this inner struggle, and reveals her wound movingly in the following poem:

I Hate Myself

Silky Smooth Flowing Hair
Soft White Skin
Snubbingly Delicate Dainty Nose
And Eyes of Birthstone Blue,

With a waist which wears ever thinner,
And a build which bears no backbone,
The model woman is everywhere.

TV, Newspapers, Magazines.
She exists in my mind, in my subconscious mind,
And she scolds my every me.

My every me is an earthly me.
It is as brown as the barren soil,
It is kinky hair and a boisterous nose,
And eyes of ever-piercing brown.

The model woman does not exist in me.
I am tangled up in black and white.
My whiteness is accepted.
My blackness is rejected.

And so you see,
I reject myself.
Subconsciously, of course.

Sometimes I think it hurts as much
as others' pain and rejection,
But then I know,
it even hurts more,

More than others' hatred and dislike,
More than others' rejection,

A PRESCRIPTION FOR THE DISEASE

for in my rejection of me,
I also reject my race.
And in my rejection of my race,
I become a racist.

A racist against my own.
What an ironic twist!
And how much more unbearable,
To be guilty of the same dislike which is aimed at me,
Which hurts me.

The people with dark skin are a part of me,
A part which I must learn to love.
In loving them, I will come to love myself.
In hating myself, I hate them as well.

And so begins my own racism,
A penetratingly painful kind.
For I begin to see how the whites can hate blacks,
and how the whites can hate me.
And I begin to see how I can hate blacks,
And how I can hate me.

6
Living a Lie

What led to the development of racism in America? The European settlers' warped view of people of color, especially the African slave. A clue to their thinking can be found in "The Federalist," a collection of eighty-five political essays written in 1787 and 1788 by three Founding Fathers, Alexander Hamilton, John Jay and James Madison. Essay number 54 defends the Constitution's proposition that the slave is only part man: "Let the compromising expedient of the Constitution be mutually adopted, which regards them (slaves) as inhabitants, but as debased by servitude below the equal level of free inhabitants; which regards the slave as divested of two fifths of the man."

What led to that type of thinking? The thoughts of highly respected men of the past who were advocates or apologists of the Europeans' enslavement of Africans. Most Americans' view of slavery was different than those in ancient Rome, Greece, Egypt, and West Africa, where slavery was an established institution. To the American owner, slaves were beasts of burden. That's what makes the slavery practiced in the United States perhaps the most bestial form of slavery in the history of humankind.

In ancient Greece, poets, novelists, playwrights and teachers were slaves. In Rome, the empire's publishing industry was run by slaves, producing about 150 books a day. Egypt at one time was ruled by slave-kings (the Mamlukes), and its armies led by slave-generals. Any slave in the Arab world who had talent could expect to advance. But the American slave was prohibited from learning how to read and write. Educating their slaves, many American slave holders felt, would be like trying to educate their cows and pigs.

The warped view of the African slave in America was held by leading clergymen in Europe as well as in the New World. For example, when a group of Portuguese entrepreneurs in 1452 decided to enslave what they called the "African pagan," they needed someone with great influence to approve of their commercial enterprise. Knowing that Pope Nicholas V believed that Africans were devoid of souls, they approached him for his blessing – and received it, with one proviso: that they Christianize the "African pagan." Rome supported the enterprise for two hundred years. The church's endorsement inspired the French, Dutch, Spanish and English to venture into slave trading.

In reality, the Africans who were being enslaved weren't pagans. Many of them were Muslims who prayed five times a day to God and lived by a strict moral code. Others practiced animism, a pantheistic religion, much like the religion of the American Indians, who believed that the Great Spirit (God) is reflected in all of life.

Neither were these West Africans savages, as their captors tried to depict them. Most of them were from highly-civilized kingdoms – Ghana, Benin, Songhay and Mali. Many African farmers were using metal plowing instruments at the time when most of their European counterparts were using sticks. Africans were leading exporters of gold, and they had commercial routes reaching into the Middle East. Ceramics and sculpting were highly developed. A flourishing textile industry existed. In Timbuktu, a center of enlightenment, Southern European scholars came to learn from black philosophers. A sophisticated system of jurisprudence was practiced in that city; young men throughout the Moslem world went to Timbuktu to study law and surgery at the University of Sankore, whose medical institute performed successful cataract removal operations, and developed an anesthetic that would keep a patient unconscious during surgery. In most of Europe, patients were knocked unconscious when undergoing surgery. A vaccination against smallpox was introduced into North America in 1721 by a slave who brought the method over from Africa.

"In Timbuktu," Leo Africanus, a Christianized Moor who visited the city in the sixteenth century, said, "there are numerous judges, doctors, and clerics, all receiving good salaries from the king. He pays great respect to men of learning. There is a big demand for books in manuscript, imported from Barbary. More profit is made from the book trade than from any other line of business."

Across the continent, Tanzanians were manufacturing carbon steel before the birth of Christ. Early Africans also built ships that could carry as much as eighty tons, one of which transported a cargo of elephants from Kenya to China in the thirteenth century.

As you can see, the religionists who believed that Africans were pagans and savages suffered from an emotional commitment to ignorance. A lot of damage was done in the name of God. For nearly two hundred years in Maryland, the Jesuits not only had slaves work their farms, they also engaged in some slave trading as well.

Prior to the formation of the United States of America, many Protestant ministers in the North and South openly preached that blacks were inherently inferior to whites, citing biblical passages as evidence. Most Puritans believed that blacks bore the curse of Cain, a sin for which their slavery was a way of atonement.

They also noted that in the Old Testament slavery was considered lawful (See Lev. 25:39-55), and that the Apostle Paul, in the New Testament, condoned slavery, declaring that when a slave disobeys his master it is like disobeying God (1 Tim. 6:2-3).

In his book, *The Invention of the Negro*, writer Earl Conrad exposes the thinking of some of the leading Puritan clergymen on the matter of race. Here he focuses on one of the most famous ministers:

> "When Cotton Mather took over his father's pulpit he was so irritated by the complete uselessness of the red man as a laborer that he couldn't conceive of the resisting Indians as being human. 'We know not when or how these Indians first became inhabitants of the mighty continent, yet we may guess that the Devil decoyed these miserable savages hither, in hope that the gospel of the Lord Jesus

54

Christ would never come to destroy or disturb his absolute empire over them.' He beheld in the kidnapped African the best hope for cheap labor and organized some Rules for the Society of Negroes in 1693, one of which was that Negroes disobedient and unfaithful to their masters must be re-buked, denied attendance at church meetings, and run-aways must be brought back to their masters and punished. In this, he said, the church was committed to implement St. Paul who had said that servants should be returned to their masters. When some members of his church bought a Negro slave for him, he declared that a 'mighty smile of heaven descended upon him.'"

In the 1730s, a leading Baptist evangelist, Dean Barkley of Rhode Island, refused to give blacks the sacraments of the church because he felt they were subhuman. Other ministers followed Barkley's lead. In 1767, several Presbyterian churches in Virginia engaged in a lucrative religious enterprise that involved the rental of slave women to plantation owners. They started out by purchasing two fertile young slave women. By 1835 they were renting out seventy. The plantation owners could do whatever they wished with the hired black women. As for the profits? They were used to pay the pastors' salaries.

There were clergymen who weren't shy about resorting to brut-ish behavior in disciplining slaves. A Virginian, Reverend Samuel Gray, recovered a runaway slave and had another slave beat the runaway to death.

Even the more liberal churches drew the color line. When a free black entered a white church, he was met at the door and ushered to a section reserved for non-whites. This practice included even the Quakers, who openly opposed slavery, but had benches set aside for blacks in their meeting halls. Most parishioners understood what the segregated seating meant: Blacks were not quite good enough, not intellectually and socially mature enough, to sit with the superior whites. Though this view was rarely stated openly, many blacks recognized the slight, and were moved to establish the black Christian church in America. Richard Allen led the way. In 1816, the African Methodist Episcopal Church was formed with Allen as bishop.

Keep in mind that from the time slaves arrived in North America, generation after generation of church-goers heard spokesmen of God talk of the inherent inferiority of blacks. And not all of the parishioners were white. It is very difficult for a religious person not to internalize what is considered divinely sanctioned. Good, hard-working men and women, as well as children, accepted as the truth the preacher's warped view of dark-skinned people, people who, in reality, were members of the human family. In those days the principles of the oneness of humankind and unity and diversity were unknown. As a consequence, the sincere God-fearing, church-going white American of the seventeenth, eighteenth, nineteenth and early twentieth centuries was unaware of having embraced a concept that generated so much suffering and misery among black men, women and children for nearly four hundred years. They were unaware of living a lie.

Members of the clergy made an organized effort to drill their warped view of Africans into the slaves. The indoctrination took place in churches built primarily for slaves and administered by white pastors. Every time blacks attended these churches, they would have to recite a special catechism that had been prepared for them:

Q. Who keeps the snakes and all bad things from hurting you?
A. God does.
Q. Who gave you a master and a mistress?
A. God gave them to me.
Q. Who says that you must obey them?
A. God says that I must.
Q. What book tells you these things?
A. The Bible.

Q. How does God do all of his work?

A. He always does it right.

Q. Does God love to work?

A. Yes, God is always at work.

Q. Do the angels work?

A. Yes, they do what God tells them.

Q. Do they love to work?

A. Yes, they love to please God.

Q. What does God say about your work?

A. He that shall not work shall not eat.

Q. Did Adam and Eve have to work?

A. Yes, they had to keep that garden.

Q. Was it hard to keep the garden?

A. No, it was very easy.

Q. What makes the crops so hard to grow now?

A. Sin makes it.

Q. What makes you lazy?

A. My wicked heart.

Q. How do you know your heart is wicked?

A. I feel it every day.

Q. Who teaches you so many wicked things?

A. The devil.

Q. Must you let the devil teach you?

A. No, I must not.

Imagine what it must have been like for the slave to recite the catechism every time he attended church services. Stripped of his rich cultural heritage, prohibited from learning how to read and write, and having never experienced freedom, he could do little to ward off the effects of the religious brainwashing technique administered by the spokesmen of God. The slave catechism had to be a factor in causing the festering wound that still plagues many African-Americans today.

Churchmen were not the only influential Americans who helped shape the prevailing white attitude toward blacks. Politicians played a significant role. As has already been pointed out, America's

Founding Fathers believed that slaves weren't fully human. Even the brilliant and highly-cultured Thomas Jefferson felt that blacks were "a form of orangutan." On the basis of this reasoning, the former president of the United states and writer of the Declaration of Independence practiced bestiality – for he had a black mistress.

Who influenced Jefferson's political and social thinking? English philosopher, John Locke, who was called "the champion of liberal enlightenment" by his peers. Locke's natural rights ideas were embodied in the Declaration of Independence. Since Locke believed that democracy was for whites and slavery for blacks, the principle that "all men are created equal," which is a pivotal part of the Declaration of Independence, wasn't meant to include blacks. That notion was certainly reinforced by the Constitution, which stated that slaves were three-fifths human.

It seems that it wasn't enough that America's most precious document had pronounced slaves less human than whites. There seemed to be a need for advocates of this point of view to continue to bombard the citizenry with what they felt was scientific data supporting their belief that blacks were inherently inferior to whites. So-called scientific studies were undertaken to prove their point. Take, for example, the study organized by Dr. Josiah C. Nott in the 1840s. The South Carolinian physician measured the heads of blacks and whites. He found that black heads were smaller than white heads, and from that finding deduced that blacks must have smaller brains and were therefore less intelligent than whites. (If the size of one's cranium determines a creature's intelligence, then elephants must be geniuses). Nott's findings were embraced by intellectuals in the North as well as the South – even in Europe. They inspired French historian/philosopher Count de Gobineau to write a book, *The Inequality of the Human Race*, which became an American best seller. University biology and anthropology courses featured Nott's views.

Though Nott's study was recognized decades later as a fraud, it, and other pseudo-scientific studies like it, added another layer of legitimacy to the prevailing view among whites that blacks were subhuman.

Harvard medical historian Allan Brandt points out that, after Nott's revelations, scientists continued to reinforce the white man's warped view of the black:

"By the turn of the century, Darwinism had provided a new rationale for American racism. Essentially primitive peoples, it was argued, could not be assimilated into a complex, white civilization. Scientists speculated that in the struggle for survival the Negro in America was doomed. Particularly prone to disease, vice and crime, black Americans could not be helped by education or philanthropy. Social Darwinists analyzed census data to predict the virtual extinction of the Negro in the twentieth century, for they believed the Negro race in America was in the throes of a degenerative evolutionary process."

Many physicians also believed that the sexual nature of blacks set them apart from whites. One doctor wrote in the Journal of the American Medical Association: "The Negro springs from a southern race, and as such his sexual appetite is strong; all of his environments stimulate this appetite, and as a general rule his emotional type of religion certainly does not decrease it."

Some well known physicians depicted black males as sexual monsters who crave white women. Brandt quotes Dr. William Lee Howard, a 19th century physician, as saying:

"The attacks on defenseless white women are evidences of racial instincts that are about as amenable to ethical culture as is the inherent odor of the race ... When education will reduce the size of the Negro's penis as well as bring about the sensitiveness of the terminal fibers which exist in the Caucasian, then will it also be able to prevent the African's birthright to sexual madness and excess."

Of course, these physicians never addressed the voracious appetite that white slave masters had for slave women. That was always a hush-hush type of activity. A quick survey of most African-American populations will reveal men and women of many different shades of brown and tan – obviously the result of black and white sexual involvement in the past, an involvement that wasn't inspired by black women, to be sure.

The U.S. Supreme Court also played a role in reinforcing the white's warped view of the black. Take the Dred Scott case in 1857, for example. In the majority opinion, Chief Justice Roger Taney stated that blacks "are not included, and were not intended to be included, in the word citizen in the Constitution ... being subordinate and inferior class of beings."

Of course, economics was a factor in reinforcing the idea that blacks weren't fully human. Though slave-rearing was never officially recognized as an industry, an industry it was. In fact, it was a $150 million industry in the early 1850s. And in those days, a dollar was worth a lot more than it is today. A change of heart toward blacks would have been costly.

To reinforce the establishment's view of blacks, whites masterfully crafted the Black Sambo image. If poorly managed, Sambo's latent bestial qualities would come to the fore, and he would become an animal in a human body, with some human capabilities making him a potential danger to the natural order. If properly trained, however, Sambo would turn into a docile, submissive figure, and, regardless of age, would always exhibit childish characteristics. As a result, many whites would have no qualms about calling a seventy-five-year-old black grandfather "boy."

The Sambo image of the black person was popularized during the early stages of the Jim Crow period. Respected writers helped to promulgate this unflattering notion of blacks. Thomas Dixon – a powerful North Carolinian preacher – was one of them. Not only was he a dynamic speaker, but he used his pen to persuade whites in the North and South that blacks were naturally incapable of assuming leadership in politics, religion, business, science and education. Though Dixon opposed slavery, he felt blacks were put on this planet to perform basic servile functions in a community, ostensibly to do the bidding of whites. His best-seller novel, *The Leopard's Spots*, makes that point in dramatic fashion. It also reinforces a certain fear that most whites still harbor, and that is, the amalgamation of the black and white races. One of the heroes of the novel, a preacher by the name of John Durham, says America would lose its high station in the world should the races mix. The character Durham, obviously reflecting Dixon's views, reveals in forceful terms what would happen if the barrier between blacks and whites broke down:

"When the white race begin to hobnob with the Negro and seek his favor, they must grant him absolute equality. That means ultimately social as well as political equality. You can't ask a man to vote for you and kick him down your front door step and tell him to come around the back way.

"... I am looking into the future. One drop of Negro blood makes a Negro. It kinks the hair, flattens the nose, thickens the lips, puts out the light of intellect, and lights the fires of brutal passions. The beginning of Negro equality as a vital fact is the beginning of the end of this nation's life. There is enough Negro blood here to make malatoo the whole republic.

"... Every inch in the approach of these races across the barriers that separate them is a movement toward death. You cannot seek the Negro vote without asking him to your home sooner or later. If you ask him to your house, he will break bread with you at last. And if you seat him at your table, he has the right to ask your daughter's hand in marriage."

Durham's solution to the problem of preventing the mixing of the races was to remove all blacks from the continent. Lifting them to the level of whites, he felt, was impossible:

"Can you change the color of his skin, the kink of his hair, the bulge of his lips, the spread of his nose, or the beat of his heart, with a spelling book? The Negro is the human donkey. You can train him, but you can't make of him a horse. Mate him with a horse, you lose the horse, and get a larger donkey called a mule, incapable of preserving his species."

Books like *The Leopard's Spots* helped to make racism a chronic disease in America. Through powerful logic, it reinforced the whites' warped view of blacks, and cleverly exploited white fears of what racial integration would lead to. One didn't have to read the book to be affected by it. Since it was so popular, magazines and newspapers reviewed it, published articles about it. It became, for a while, a favorite topic of discussion. Its impact wasn't confined to the period in which the book was published (1902). It indirectly affected the generations that followed. Parents have a way of inculcating their strongest feelings and views in their children.

The roots of race prejudice toward African-Americans are deep – and as vital as ever. Nourishing them over the years were the attitudes and behavior of powerful clergymen, business tycoons, politicians, judges, writers and professors who helped to shape the national mind-set on race. Their influence was so great that whatever changes were instituted in trying to overcome racism were superficial. The core problem still exists, the feeling among whites that blacks are inherently inferior. Because most whites today know that racism is wrong, they arm themselves with sophisticated ways of masking their racial feelings. What is sad is that those who want to rid themselves of those feelings don't know where to turn for help. When you consider the role that religion, politics, the judiciary, the intelligentsia and economics played for hundreds of years in shaping the white person's attitude toward blacks, you can appreciate why it's so difficult to rid oneself of the prejudice. It is ingrained in the consciousness of the white man and woman.

Even President Abraham Lincoln, who freed the four million slaves, wasn't free of the prejudice; nor were many of the abolitionists. Lincoln, in fact, had no plans or ideas for integrating the freed slave into the mainstream of American society. His initial impulse was either to ship all blacks back to Africa, or carve out a colony for them in Central America. That impulse was based on a belief that blacks were incapable of living with whites on an equal basis. Lincoln was not alone in that belief. Thousands of Northern soldiers, who were opposed to slavery and fought in the Civil War, had never rid themselves of the prevailing and warped white view that blacks were inferior.

After the Civil War, most whites showed little compassion for the freed slaves who had been set loose to live in a world they had not been prepared for. Whites in both the North and South quickly came to the conclusion that their fundamental feelings about blacks were justified, when they saw the ex-slaves awkwardly trying to adapt to the white man's world. The unfair struggle gave whites cause to believe that blacks were incapable of living in a civilized society.

The passage by Congress of the Fourteenth Amendment to the Constitution, which eliminated the "three-fifths" clause, failed to eliminate the belief of many whites that blacks were not fully human, however. The pattern of racial thinking had been set.

Some people feel that those who opposed slavery weren't infected by the disease of racism. Not so. Some fought slavery because they didn't like to see any living creature in bondage. In fact, they may have loved free or enslaved blacks, and still harbored an inherent feeling of superiority toward them, incapable of accepting them as their equal.

I'll never forget the time – in Kansas City – of being confronted by a black man on this issue. While speaking about the importance of loving one another as a means of overcoming racism, I noticed a man in the audience raise his hand. At first, I ignored him. But he was persistent. About five minutes later, he stood up, his hand still raised. At the time, I was annoyed, for I was on a roll. Finally, I acknowledged him, hoping he would be brief.

He was brief all right – but profound. And today I am glad he spoke up, for he revealed to me something I never considered before.

"Sir," he said, "Love is not enough in creating racial unity. Respect is required. You can love your dog, but you'll never consider him your equal. First, I want your respect, then you can love me."

As long as whites harbor an inherent feeling of superiority they will be incapable of affording a black person the respect he or she deserves as a fellow human being. The disrespect is manifested even in places where you wouldn't expect it.

I witnessed a flagrant example of this on the Oprah Winfrey television show. Though Oprah, who hosts the show, is black, she was unable to prevent it from happening. She eventually put a stop to it, but the damage had already been done.

The theme of the show that day was how white-collar couples cope with unemployment. On the panel were two couples, one black, the other white. Both men had held high-powered managerial jobs. Two experts – both white – were also on the panel. After explaining their situation, the black couple had little to say. Not because they didn't want to share more. The experts, who seemed sympathetic, were so condescending to the blacks that they withdrew psychologically from the conversation. When the camera zeroed in on them, I noticed the black man gritting his teeth and squeezing his wife's hand. Aware of what was happening, Oprah cut off one of the experts and tried to solicit comments from the black panelists. By then, it was too late. The experts, meanwhile, were unaware of the pain they had caused the black couple.

I was able to detect the unconscious disrespect shown the blacks on the television show, because I had done what those experts did. In my case, however, a friend caught me doing it.

The friend – a black woman – and I were doing a racism workshop together. Without really consulting her, I organized a schedule which had me speaking first. I never revealed to her why I should function as the keynoter. But she knew why I took the dominant role: I felt I had more significant things to share with the audience than she did. My decision wasn't based on objective evidence. My friend didn't make an issue of it that day. But after some serious soul searching that night, she rocked me and the audience with personal feelings most people would never reveal. She said she had to do what she did not only to recapture her self-respect, but to help me.

When she opened her statement with, "Nathan hurt me yesterday," I felt betrayed, hurt, bewildered, and fearful of what she was about to say.

"I know," she declared, "that Nathan was unaware of the pain he had inflicted on me yesterday. Though I have endured that kind of pain before, it still hurts, and I never get used to it."

At that point I felt psychologically exposed – with every eye in the room glaring at me.

"Nathan organized the speaking schedule last night without consulting with me. He told me what the order was, and I like a fool went along with it. As soon as I consented to the secondary role, doubts about my ability to perform last night overwhelmed me. I found myself in Nathan's shadow – his inferior. As he spoke, I grew less and less sure of myself."

My initial reaction was to strike back, to defend my reputation, protect my pride. Fortunately, I kept my mouth shut – and listened to my friend continue to share what was in her heavy heart:

"I vowed several years ago that I would never let what happened to me last night happen again. As I speak, I sense I'm regaining my confidence, chasing away those doubts that have haunted me ever since I was a little child. They don't seem to go away. What I have been able to do, however, is to distance myself from those negative feelings about myself. But that takes continuous effort on my part. There are times like yesterday, however, when I am caught off guard, and become less of what I really am.

"Right now – I feel better," she said, looking at me. "I won't allow Nathan to do to me what he did yesterday."

After pausing a moment and still peering at me, she added, "I feel confident that Nathan can take what I have dished out. He understands."

Her last remark helped me to break out of the mental cage of self-pity I had constructed; I was ready to want to understand what she had shared with everyone in the workshop. In time, the understanding came to me.

T hat experience has made me more sensitive in my interpersonal relations with African-Americans, but it didn't heal my infection. Just as my friend has to work continually at warding off the doubts that have plagued her since childhood, I must do the same thing to keep my infection from flaring up. And it doesn't matter that I have become quite knowledgeable about many different facets of racism, that I am actively combating it, that I am committed to the cause of racial unity, and that one of the principles of my faith calls for the abolition of all prejudices.

Though I have made some progress in overcoming this social sickness, *the fact remains that I'm still infected.* Whatever advancement I have made is due to my faith's demand of me to free myself of racism. I pray every day for help; and that fuels my resolve to heal this disease that for a long time I never knew I had. Knowing the nature of the illness has also been helpful in combating it. For without that knowledge I wouldn't know how to go about curing myself. An accurate diagnosis is the first step to healing a sickness.

7
Basic Feelings

I think most people will agree that, in order to solve a problem, an understanding of the nature of the problem is necessary. Otherwise, inappropriate solutions will be devised, and the problem will persist – and most likely worsen.

No sane person will reject the notion that racism is a problem. Unfortunately, proposed solutions have been developed over the years which, frankly, haven't worked very well. The track record is so feeble that most people – black and white – feel that finding a solution is impossible. As a result, cynicism has become another obstacle in the search for a solution.

The key to finding a solution to racism is gaining an accurate understanding of its nature. That isn't as easy as it seems. For the first step in the process is a genuine desire to gain the understanding. So many men and women of good will who suffer from denial are afraid to make the search. They are afraid, because deep down they suspect what they'll find, and won't know how to cope with it.

Through reading, attending lectures, interviewing behavioral scientists, and engaging in some serious soul-searching, I discovered – to my horror – that I was infected by racism. And after further inquiry I realized that racism is a disease that has grown into an epidemic, spreading throughout North America and infecting and wounding almost everyone in its path. The disease has festered, virtually unchecked, for nearly four hundred years, with attention given primarily to its symptoms, which have been mistaken for the problem. A costly mistake when you consider the damage done over the centuries.

A disease doesn't have to be a physical ailment. Webster's Third

International Dictionary defines it as a lack of ease: discomfort, distress, and trouble. There is no question that racism has caused a lack of ease, discomfort for the individual and community, distress and trouble. And disease is also defined as "an inherent defect of an organism."

What is the defect in relation to racism? It's certainly not a bacterial or viral infection, but, rather, a psychological disorder. Those of us who suffer from this malady have a distorted perception of an aspect of reality – the nature of the black person – that has evolved into a deep compulsion, similar to what drives an alcoholic. When an alcoholic sees a bottle of whiskey, a certain feeling comes over him which he has difficulty controlling. He wants to consume the contents of the bottle. How much control he's able to display depends on how bad his condition is. Even if he's able to resist taking a drink, but experiences that compulsion, he's still considered an alcoholic.

The same is true when most whites find themselves in the midst of blacks. Feelings and perceptions well up in them that they don't experience when with other whites. Basically, there's a sense of uneasiness, ranging from guilt to raw hostility. How uneasy they feel depends on how severe the disorder.

Not everyone who suffers from this disease is a bigot, someone who flaunts his racism and is willing to express his feelings violently, the way a group of New York City white youths did recently. They attacked two black youths who were on their way home from school. After pummeling them, the assailants sprayed the black youngsters' faces and hands with white paint and said, "Now you can amount to something."

Most whites who suffer from the disease of racism don't resort to that type of behavior. In fact, while in the company of African-Americans, they'll try to hide their revulsion that stems from inherent feelings of superiority. Some whites have become skillful at masking their true feelings, and perform like seasoned diplomats. By attending tolerance and diversity workshops they have learned how to interact with blacks in a civil manner, making sure never to say or do the wrong thing. While no outward friction results from such encounters, many blacks shy away from being with those whites again, for they intuitively sense the whites' true feelings. Those whites, meanwhile, continue to align themselves with various human rights causes, and work hard at giving the impression that they're free of racial prejudice.

Denial is a pathetic state of mind. Because so many whites who suffer from denial can distinguish between what is right and wrong, and they know it is wrong to harbor racist feelings, to be identified with a patent evil, they pretend to be free of any race prejudice. Some know that they are lying to themselves, while others have consciously blocked out the truth. They are in a dilemma, because they want desperately to do the right thing. Those who are lying to themselves feel it is the only rational thing they can do, for there is no one they can turn to for help. Oftentimes those who would offer to help are in denial themselves. The best they can do is provide alternative escapist solutions that end up numbing one's conscience. Finding blame outside of themselves is a favorite escape route. They are usually among the first to brand a poor Southern white person a "redneck."

Some find escape by becoming actively involved in as much civil rights work as possible. It is their way of proclaiming to the community that they are free of racism. In some cases, they'll marry a black person to make their point. Such activity eases the pain that the lie produces and reinforces the blockage.

Because most of those who suffer from denial are sensitive about race issues, they tend to avoid racial confrontations and become extremely defensive when pressed into them. This was apparent at a meeting I was asked to moderate for a group in the Pacific Northwest. Most of the blacks, Asians and whites who belonged to the human rights organization wanted to establish an Institute for the Healing of Racism in their city.

Everyone agreed on the ground rules listed in the Institute's brochure. But when we began to discuss them, some people expressed reservations. A middle-aged black woman, who ignited fear in many of the whites whenever she spoke, was upset. "When I tried to set up something like the Institute for the Healing of Racism six months ago, very few members of the organization participated," she said. "Now about thirty have registered, because some sweet-talking white dude comes here with a plan that he says has a fine track record. Well, as far as I'm concerned, he isn't coming up with something new."

The president of the group, a woman of Irish Catholic background, interrupted the black woman: "Look – why drag up what happened in the past. We're making a fresh beginning."

"Look here, time is not what concerns me," the black woman said.

"What concerns you?"

"Justice."

"We're all concerned with justice, or we wouldn't be members of this organization."

The black woman's eyes were blazing. "I'm not talking about some pie-in-the-sky justice," she said, poking her chest with a forefinger. "I'm talking about the injustices directed at me – by the leadership of this so-called human rights organization."

Some of the members started squirming in their seats. The president flushed, struggling not to lash back. "Now let's not get angry," she said, writing something on a yellow pad.

"I'm not only angry," the black woman said. "I'm pissed off – sick and tired of your goody-two-shoes attitude. For years I stayed in the background taking a lot of racist crap from you people, so that I would be accepted. Because I rarely challenged what you people decided to do, I was an okay black.

"Believe me, I was angry then – but a fool, full of fear of upsetting you people's feelings, and afraid of not being accepted. But now – I'm still angry, but no longer willing to hide it. Only a bullet is going to stop me from telling it the way it is.

"If I were white and had set up what I set up six months ago, most of you would have attended our meetings. I sent out invitations, called people, bought and baked snacks and scrubbed the apartment spotless every Thursday night for three months, and the same four people showed up, three blacks and an Asian. Not one white face."

She pointed at the president and shouted, "You promised to come, but at the last minute you'd come up with some lame excuse why you couldn't make it."

The president, still flushed, kept writing on her pad, obviously preparing a response to the accusations being hurled at her.

"You're a damn phony," the black woman continued. "You give beautiful speeches about human rights, with fancy quotes and clever metaphors, but you never once offered to drive me home. You know I don't have a car, and that for me to make our meetings I have to take three different buses – an hour-and-a-half trip each way. If it wasn't for the brothers here I would have had to go home in the rain, alone, lots of times. You didn't offer to take me home, because I don't count, I have no clout, just another pitiful black bitch loudmouth who's always stirring up trouble."

Pounding on the table, she shouted, "Well I'm going to continue to stir up trouble until you admit what you really are – racist to the core.

"You don't want to come to my home, especially at night, because I live in the ghetto. You're afraid of being mugged. You think I live in a rat- and roach-infested place. At least, say how you really feel. But you don't. You lie to me and you lie to yourself.

"And you never once – in the five years I've been coming to these meetings – invited me to your house. Not once – like I'm some kind of diseased creature. Almost every other white in this room has been to your house."

"Now wait a minute!" said the president. "I've had it with your groundless accusations."

"First of all," she said, her eyes riveted on the pad, "I could never make it to your meetings, because they were during the week. I have three small children and a husband to care for."

"That's a bunch of bullshit," the black woman countered. "I know you go other places during the week."

"How do you know? You have spies?"

"I know!" the black woman shouted.

The president waved in disgust at her accuser, and continued to read from her pad as fast as she could to prevent the black woman from interrupting her: "I invited you and everyone else to the fundraiser barbecue at my house last summer. You didn't show up, and didn't have the decency to call me to let me know you weren't coming.

"You say I'm a phony do-gooder. I don't remember you saying that when I got you the job you hold now. You were unemployed, and I literally made more than fifty calls to set up interviews for you. Never once did you show any appreciation for what I've done for you.

"The way I'm rewarded for doing you a good deed is to be the target of your backbiting."

The president looked at the black woman. "You think blacks are the only ones who are treated unfairly. What about my people? I remember my great-grandmother telling me how her mother was ostracized by students at the high school she attended in Boston because she was Irish and Catholic. While looking for a job, she was often greeted by signs reading, 'Irish need not apply.' She had to clean toilet bowls for a living."

"The Ku Klux Klan didn't only hound blacks. They hounded Catholics, too, burning our churches in the North and South."

Tears started to well up in the president's eyes. "One of my cousins was killed by a Protestant sniper in Londonderry two years ago because he was believed to be an advocate of a united Ireland."

Crying, the president stood up. "I hurt, too. My people have suffered, too. But we don't allow our pain to consume us.

"I'm fed up with your rage, with your bullying tactics. I don't want anything to do with you – or any organization that you're a part of."

The president stormed out of the room, sobbing uncontrollably.

I was saddened by what I had just witnessed: both women, in pain, victims of racism, and unable to work together for a cause they both believe in.

Watching the argument taught me something. Had the president not been in denial, had she been truthful in her response, the fire in the black woman would have been extinguished. In her charges, the black woman invited the president to be truthful, but she refused the invitation, responding with a defense that turned into a counterattack meant to keep others from learning her true feelings toward blacks.

Instead of listening with the heart, as well as the ear, to what the black woman was saying, the president took careful notes, with the intent of refuting every charge made by her attacker. She was more concerned with concealing her secret and achieving victory than gaining understanding.

Had she truly heard the black woman, the president would have discerned the reason for her rage. But that's impossible to do when you're busy defending yourself.

One of the things I have learned in the past three years is that a black person will reach out to a white person who is sincere, genuine and truthful about his infection. A bridge of understanding between the two will eventually emerge. Sincerity, genuineness and truthfulness are more important than being culturally attuned to the ways of blacks. The state of one's heart is more important than knowing what is culturally correct in terms of speech and actions. The latter can be attained in time through association with blacks, but the former is achieved by developing a pure heart, free of self-deception – and a willingness to heal one's infection. The catch is, without a pure heart the chances of associating with blacks are slim, and learning to be culturally smart among blacks would have to come through human relations seminars and workshops, where developing a pure heart is rarely stressed. On the basis of personal experience, I know that being sincere, genuine, and honest about one's infection will change an angry black person's view of a white person.

There have been a number of experiences, but the one that touched me the most occurred at a university in Texas. A lot had to be crammed into an eight-hour period. Three speaking engagements; meetings with a professor and a graduate student; and an interview with a newspaper reporter.

My first encounter with Steve was at the African-American history class I addressed. After my talk, he tested my sincerity. Sitting in the back row, wearing a dark gray cap and a black shirt, he directed a question at me that had nothing to do with what I had shared with the class:

"Do you sleep well at night?"

"Yes, I do. I have no trouble sleeping."

Steve leaned forward and said, "But I can't sleep well."

"I think I know why."

"How can you stand there – a white man – and tell me you know why I can't sleep well? You have no idea how I feel about myself – a black man trying to make it in a racist society."

I looked Steve straight in the eye. "True – I can't feel your pain; I haven't experienced your rejection. But I have made an effort to understand what has caused the hostility that African-Americans must face in our land. And I've tried to determine how I have contributed to the maintenance of racism in America."

At that point, the professor cut me off. Pointing to the clock on the wall, he reminded the students that the class period was over. As we filed out of the room, Steve avoided me, didn't even look my way.

An hour later, he was in a small auditorium to hear my second presentation. By then I had learned that Steve, a reporter for the student newspaper, was considered one of the most militant black leaders on campus. This time he didn't ask any questions. He left without acknowledging my glances toward him. Frankly, I was surprised when he showed up in the big auditorium. He was with some of his friends. Though there were many dignitaries in the audience, including the editor of the city newspaper, professors, university administrators and leaders of the black community, my address was directed to Steve that evening. I shared how I discovered my infection and how I have struggled to heal myself.

After the talk, many in the audience – black and white – approached me. Steve was among them. I could tell he had been moved; there were tears in his eyes. We did what our hearts compelled us to do – we embraced. After thanking me for coming, he asked whether, in his role as reporter, he could interview me the following day.

While we met the next day, there wasn't much of an interview. Five minutes into the interview, Steve put his pencil down, and we talked for close to two hours. He opened his heart, sharing with me his background, his frustrations, his pain, his dreams and the wounds that the victims of racism usually bear. He told me things that, he said, he had never shared with some of his closest friends. It was painful to hear him talk about the doubts he had about his ability to be what he wanted to be. To me the obstacles he talked about were surmountable. I knew what I would do to gain what I wanted. But then again, I was white, with certain built-in advantages in our society that many blacks don't enjoy. No amount of sermonizing by me was going to remove the doubts that were plaguing him. I did, however, offer some suggestions on how he could refine his writing skills. Steve wanted to be a writer.

Shortly before we said goodbye, Steve looked at me and said, with a sincerity that springs from one's soul, "I want you to know that I consider you like my father."

"And you are my son," I said.

A year later, I learned that Steve had written a play about racism that was performed at his university, winning wide acclaim.

When a white person refuses to recognize that he's infected by the disease of racism, he stands the risk of being reminded of his infection – which can be a painful experience, especially for someone who wants desperately to be free of his racist feelings. Stress usually causes the infection to flare up. Unless one becomes a monk or hermit, the kind of stress that sets off the flare-up is practically impossible to avoid. And being a liberal won't prevent this from happening.

I remember what it is like. Years ago, while walking down the street one day, I noticed an interracial couple approaching me, the black man holding the white woman's hand. My immediate reaction was revulsion. I had no idea of where that odious feeling came from.

The fact that I didn't want to feel that way didn't help. The fact that I knew it was wrong to feel that way only compounded my dilemma. In self-defense, I looked away from the couple, trying to compose myself. Perhaps, I thought, I could chase away that horrible feeling with a positive thought. I looked at the interracial couple again, forced a smile and said to myself, "That's perfectly normal, and that's the way it should be."

It didn't work. The feeling of revulsion remained, as strong as before. The so-called positive thought was no match for the feeling that seemed to dominate my entire being. I had said the right thing to myself, but deep down I didn't believe it. Horrified that I could feel that way, I looked away from the couple again, and resorted to what I had done in the past under similar circumstances: I repressed the feeling. How did I do that? Since it was lunch time, I created a mental picture of one of my favorite foods – a hotdog with mustard and sauerkraut – and stayed focused on it.

I never saw the interracial couple pass me by. Moments later the revulsion was gone and I had fooled myself into believing that it would never return. What actually happened was that that feeling returned to a state of festering in my unconscious, ready to spring forth under stress brought on by another racial encounter.

The feelings revealed are not unique to these episodes. If blacks work or live among whites, especially in the North, they face denial daily. They are exposed to a variety of forms of denial, some of them so convoluted that even the most sensitive white human rights workers are unable to detect them in others, never mind themselves. They're incapable of detecting them, because denial is a carefully concealed mental maneuver, a sudden subconscious adjustment sparked by a fear of harboring prejudice that a part of you feels is wrong.

While exploring the anatomy of denial is a painstaking task, one thing is clear: Denial, in and of itself, isn't a negative psychological reflex, for it springs from a sense of shame, a desire to conceal a feeling that a person knows deep-down is socially incorrect. The thought that ridding oneself of it is an impossibility, encourages more and more repression of the feeling; an action that makes healing more and more difficult – for the deeper the hole, the tougher it is to emerge from it.

No one talks about the problem, because discussion would only exacerbate the black-white conflict. Blacks would be accused of making unfounded accusations and the whites' defensive reaction would reinforce the blacks' sense of hopelessness. So, everyone avoids the subject, creating, at best, an uneasy truce – which, in the end, only prolongs the time when the scab of denial must be torn away in order to expose the messy truth.

I know what it feels like to suffer from denial. When I finally understood my racist attitude after a series of negative reactions to blacks, I felt like a convicted criminal – standing before a judge, waiting to be sentenced. Shamed by the feeling, I tried to convince myself that my repulsion was a distortion of reality, a mirage. In self defense, I paraded all of my liberal credentials before my inner eye and convinced myself that I couldn't possibly have those feelings I sensed during that stressful moment.

$\mathbf{B}$ecause many blacks have been conditioned since childhood to survive in an alien society, they have, over the years, grown sensitive to white people's attitudes towards them. They have been exposed to an assortment of expressions of denial. The following is a list of some of the most commonly-used expressions by individuals and institutions. An African-American friend of mine, Bernard Streets, a retired microbiologist who is now a speaker on race relations, has shared with me some common expressions of denial that he's been exposed to:

1. The person who consistently tells ethnic jokes and uses in private, with close friends and associates, slanderous racial and ethnic terms – but denies that he is prejudiced on the grounds that "some of my best friends are black, Hispanic, Asian, Jewish."

2. The person who, when imitating a black, will always use a

grammatically incorrect "Negro dialect" – even if that black person is a well-known personality who does not speak that way. The imitator denies that he's prejudiced – he's just being funny.

3. The person who uses such expressions as: "John Doe is a good black person," "You people," or, "Joe, how do black people feel about such and such?" (The tendency to view every black person as a spokesperson for his race.) For example, when Streets was at Fort Sam Houston, Texas many years ago, his first sergeant was preparing his company to meet its commander. He said, "In a few minutes you'll be meeting our company commander, Captain Henry Gaskins. He's colored, but he's okay."

4. The assumption that blacks are of a different emotional make-up than whites and should be separated. For example, a white soldier in Streets' unit told him that the principal reason for separate black and white churches was that blacks were a "different temperament" and not like white folks.

5. The white person's silent opinion of "Negroid" physical features as being less attractive and more animal-like (or "apish"). The assumption here is that "white" is "normal" physiognomy – not only the standard, but the ideal.

6. Comments by whites which are condescending or pompous, indicating that they have all the answers to a minority person's problems and that these problems can be very easily solved. One example is the analogy of the white immigrant: "My grandparents came here from Ireland during the potato famine with nothing but the clothes on their backs. They worked hard, saved money, made something of their lives, educated their children and succeeded professionally. The blacks could do the same thing if they just wanted to."

The denial here is failure to see and understand the different circumstances between an immigrant who has chosen to come on his own, is white and assimilates easily, and a slave brought against his will, who, because he is black, is despised and looked upon as an animal. It's not hard to figure out which newcomer (and his descendants) will get a better break.

7. Changes in facial expressions, body language, reflexes and emotions by whites whenever a person of color appears in their presence. At a seminar on prejudice and racism, a courageous white woman shared this story about the unconscious racism she observed in herself: Well-educated and upper-middle-class, she was driving down one of Greenwich, Connecticut's main avenues at noontime. She had to stop at an intersection because the traffic light had turned red. Beautiful, majestic Greenwich High School sat on a hill to her right. Many people, including high school students, were crossing in front of her. All were white except for one, a nicely-dressed, young black man. As he crossed the street, she automatically reached over and locked all her doors. When he passed in front of her, he smiled and waved. She froze in panic. "How dare he," she thought. Then, as if hit by a Mack truck, she recognized the young man: He was a close high school chum of her son. She waved back. When the light turned green, she pulled over to the curb and sobbed uncontrollably, thinking how hurt her son's friend would be had he known of her actions. She realized immediately that she had been denying her own racism. Interestingly, after hearing her story, the people of color at the seminar showered her with hugs, kisses and affection.

W hen a person finally frees himself from the vise of denial, he is able to identify it in others and appreciate the strain and pain that blacks must endure, even in the mundane matter of finding adequate housing. A friend of mine who owns two rental properties witnessed behavior by both blacks and whites that he would never have noticed had he not broken out of the hard shell of denial. He learned a great deal when he rented the two apartments, located in a predominantly white neighborhood, to black families:

"My wife received a call from the woman who lived next door to one of the houses," he said. "We had been friendly with this woman, because we once lived in that two-family house that we were now renting out. She asked my wife, 'Am I to understand that I'm going to have black neighbors?'

"'Yes,' my wife said.

"'I see,' said our neighbor, and hung up."

My friend continued: "But that kind of bigotry is easier to handle – at least if it's honest. What made me feel worse was when my second floor tenants, two young white professional women, called and told me they were moving. It just so happened to be only days after the black family moved in. They said they had found a more modern apartment with a pool. But the new apartment was more expensive, and I knew it was further from where they worked. I knew why they were really moving, and it made me sick to my stomach.

"When my new black tenant found out they'd be moving, she said innocently, 'Oh, that's too bad – I never got a chance to get to know them.'

"The woman next door doesn't talk to me anymore, and I've sensed hostility from others on the street. I feel tension every time I visit the house. When my wife told me she had a new tenant for the second floor and that she, too, was black, I thought, to my own consternation, 'Oh, no, not again!' I was concerned about what the neighbors would think. Privately, I was hoping she would be light-skinned. And when I met her, and saw that she was light-skinned, I felt relieved, but ashamed that I felt that way."

Another form of denial among some whites is their "colorblindness." They claim they see no differences between blacks, Asians, whites, Latinos and American Indians. I can understand why they reject what their senses pick up. It is an attempt to convince themselves that all humans were created equal. But in most instances it isn't something they really believe – it is an attempt to hide a feeling they know is wrong and are incapable of overcoming. Unfortunately, they pass on their "colorblindness" to their children, thinking that will prevent them from becoming racists. While that's a nice gesture, it creates more harm than good. It generates inner conflicts in children. On the one hand, they want to comply with their parents' wishes. On the other, they notice the differences at school, in the stores and on the streets, and on television.

What will cure "colorblindness" is an understanding of the principle of unity in diversity, which was covered earlier in the book. That understanding leads to the realization that differences aren't bad, that they are part of the natural order of things; that different skin color doesn't negate, in any way, the reality of the oneness of humanity; that life was meant to be a beautiful mosaic, not all-black or all-white. God loves variety as well as unity.

In order to eradicate racism, we need to zero in on the heart of the problem – those terrible feelings that so many of us harbor, but are afraid to acknowledge. Certainly, the bigot doesn't try to hide that feeling. But bigots are not as dangerous as those of us who suffer from denial. Relatively speaking, there are only a handful of bigots, and most of them belong to extremist organizations like the Ku Klux Klan, the Skinheads and the neo-Nazis, groups that are viewed by most people as teetering on the edge of civilized behavior. It isn't that these folks are harmless. They can kill a person or two, blow up a house, terrorize neighborhoods with their strange costumes and rituals. But the great mass of whites are a greater danger to the health of a multicultural society, for their racism is more difficult to detect – because of denial and the great effort put forth to hide the symptoms of the disease. In a way, they're like an invisible, odorless, poisonous gas that, little by little, cripples and wounds people of color every day. Many blacks know this, and, until recently, have been helpless in effectively defending themselves from it. The nature of the damage done to blacks in particular will be described later in the book.

Now, I don't want to give the impression that I'm opposed to diversity sensitivity training. That's important work. But what's more important, I feel, is working at purging our hearts of the stuff that triggers racist thoughts and racist actions that we don't recognize as being racist – in other words, drawing to the conscious what's

81

festering in the unconscious. By doing that, a person becomes acquainted with his disease, wants to cure it and drafts a healing strategy. Once he's on that path, blacks won't avoid him. On the contrary, they'll find his sincerity, genuineness and honesty refreshing, and will even offer a helping hand. True friendships will develop; and cultural blunders made by the healing white person won't be held against him. He'll learn through association with blacks how to avoid making those innocent mistakes. I know this, because I've experienced it. A blunder on my part would set off lots of laughter instead of anger. Why? Because the blacks who were present knew what was in my heart.

Most psychiatrists believe that hiding the truth from oneself can be harmful. I asked a friend, Dr. John Woodall, a psychiatrist on the faculty of Harvard University Medical School and an expert in conflict resolution, for his comments on this aspect of racism. He said, in part, in his letter of reply:

"Freud stated that the purpose of psychoanalysis was to 'make the unconscious, conscious.' In other words, the goal of psychoanalysis is to bring to conscious awareness all those patterns of thinking and behaving that go unexamined. Once this is done, one can exercise free will to liberate oneself from patterns of thinking which are dysfunctional or hinder one's growth and happiness. This goal, too, reflects the admonition of Socrates that 'the unexamined life is not worth living.'

"The irony of human nature is that the very capacity for rational thought that can liberate one's life can also fall prey to irrational prejudice and blind imitation. Psychiatrists have long recognized the tendency to label one set of people as an 'in group,' and another as an 'out group.' This process of identification of good and bad groups serves to empower an individual in the face of stress. On an internal psychological level, individuals tend to place the negative parts of their own selves, their fears, anger, even the unwanted negative parts of their own secret personality, onto someone else. This tendency is called 'projection,' and it is considered a primitive defense mechanism of the mind to protect it from unpleasant experiences. In this case, the unpleasant experience is the pain felt by examining oneself to find undesirable things.

"Projection is a primitive defense against psychological pain in that it does not allow oneself to employ all the faculties of reason to investigate reality as it is. Instead, with projection, the mind labels situations and people in predetermined patterns in order to avoid the discomfort of honest and mature dealings with life. This blind imitation of old patterns of thought is ultimately dysfunctional in that one will make decisions and then act based on faulty information. The mind will have been imprisoned by its own primitive tendency to project. It is this process of projection which underlies all prejudice. And, it is the primitive dysfunctional nature of projection that classifies prejudice as a disease of the mind."

It is apparent that those who promulgated racism in the early days of America projected upon blacks those traits they found objectionable in themselves: laziness, an inordinate desire for sex, ignorance, sloppiness, deception and a lack of conscience. While whites didn't talk about engaging in such psychological maneuvering, they found it convenient to use blacks as scapegoats. Whites, who have always wielded the power in America, made sure that they were the '"in group," and blacks, the '"out group." Most whites felt comfortable with this social arrangement, and as a result, imitated blindly what was considered the race relations norm. It is a legacy whose influence remains as strong today among whites as it did in the past. The civil rights reforms, over the years, have done little to change most white people's basic feelings towards blacks.

8
Life is Unfair

For many African-Americans, life is uneven, unfair. It's a constant tease, because they see the precious possibilities acted out by white folks in the suburbs, on TV and in the movies. Living in a comfortable home in a neighborhood of their choice, or walking into a downtown store, free of fear of being scrutinized by an employee who sees them as potential criminals, are possibilities that seem beyond their grasp. It doesn't matter how much they try; attaining the freedom the white man enjoys remains elusive, regardless of economic success or professional prominence.

Philip, who is black, is a highly-respected teacher. He and his white wife – also a teacher – own a neat home on a pleasant, integrated street, and are the proud parents of a five-year-old black child they adopted as an infant in Brazil.

Outwardly, they seem self-assured. Both parents are handsome, and their daughter, everyone agrees, is a "living doll." Philip and Olive have master's degrees, are musical and are avid readers, and their child shows signs of brilliance in school. Everyone who meets them agrees that they are an extremely attractive family.

But what most acquaintances don't know is that they are a troubled family. Their problems don't stem from a bad husband-wife relationship. They remain deeply in love.

Racism is making life painful. And, in this land, there's no escape, they believe, from the pain, even for Olive, despite her whiteness. Watching her husband and daughter suffer, and being unable to relieve their suffering, is difficult to take. She shares their pain, and knows that the pressure that results from racism won't end soon. As a consequence, she's spearheading a campaign to find employment outside America, in a place where racial diversity is treated as a virtue, not a social blemish. She doesn't want her daughter coming home from school again, crying, "Mommy, they called me nigger baby," and asking, "Why do they do that?"

Philip has mixed feelings about his wife's campaign. While leaving the country would relieve a lot of personal pressure, he doesn't want to quit the fight against racism, which he feels must be fought. He never was a quitter. Yet, there are his wife and child to consider. Does he have the right to lead them into the caldron of martyrdom?

To survive in America, Philip has had to employ a dual consciousness. In the presence of whites, whether it be in the neighborhood or at work, he has had to make sure that he doesn't offend anyone, that he says what he thinks the white folks want to hear. For sharing his true feelings could mean losing his job and destroying friendships. He has had to resort to that kind of thinking so much of the time that, for a while, he lost touch with his true self.

When he realized, during a moment of deep reflection, what was happening to him, he grew angry, and over time the anger grew, especially when he was forced to mask his feelings among whites. Yet, he was careful not to reveal the anger, especially in mixed company.

Olive is aware of her husband's emotional state and his daily struggle to keep from exploding, another reason why she wants to leave the country.

Now that Philip acknowledges his anger, he's able to recall, and not repress, his introduction to racism. Though his parents tried hard to protect him and their other children from the effects of the disease, they were unable to hide what they couldn't control.

Philip was eight when the family went to Mississippi to spend the summer in the community where his parents grew up. His mother and father still had family living there.

One hot, muggy evening his mother came out of her bedroom clutching her abdomen, blood splattered over her dress. Falling to the couch, she cried out, "I'm miscarriaging!" When Philip's father called the hospital, asking for an ambulance to come fetch his bleeding wife, he was told, "Our hospital doesn't serve colored folks, but we'll try to find you some help."

Philip remembers that about an hour later, a hearse arrived, owned by the black mortician in town. "They probably thought my mother would die, but somehow she survived," he said.

That summer Philip was introduced to racial terrorism. As much as he tried, he could never drive the incident out of his mind. It seemed permanently fixed in his brain, popping into his consciousness whenever he encountered an overt or covert racist act directed against him or someone else.

Shortly after supper one night, Philip spotted two pickup trucks with men dressed in strange white costumes parked on the front lawn. With wide eyes, he watched the men approach the porch.

"Daddy," Philip called out, "are those clowns?"

The father grabbed his son's arm and pulled him away from the window. "You stay there," he shouted, pointing to the farthest corner of the parlor, where the boy's mother and younger brothers were already huddled together.

After three raps, the father opened the front door and walked onto the porch. As soon as the door closed, Philip dashed to the window and watched one of the hooded men waving his fist in his father's face. The others planted a large wooden cross on the lawn and torched it.

Two days later the family went home to California. Philip's father refused to talk to his children about that incident.

But California isn't immune to racism. It's there, too, and Philip knows that. So does Jimmie, a native Tennessean, who left for the West Coast to live in what he thought would be a less oppressive environment. Little did he know that, after he moved to California, one of the most socially progressive states in the union, he would endure the most humiliating and cruel experience of his life.

Though happily married to a white woman, Jimmie didn't turn his back on his heritage. He was actively involved in the black community. Not only did Jimmie live there, he was viewed as a leader, always organizing programs for those who needed material help, more education or an inoculation of hope. An accomplished artist, he gave children free art lessons.

Jimmie loved basketball, and every Sunday morning he would go to the park and play some "hoop" with a group of young men around his age. One Sunday he arrived a little early and decided to stay in the car and read. He was so absorbed in his book, he didn't notice the policeman approaching. A knock on the windshield caught Jimmie's attention.

"Hey, there," the policemen said, "hand me your driver's license and registration."

"What for?"

"Because I said so."

"I'm not giving you anything, because I've done nothing wrong."

"Don't sass me."

"I'm not sassing you. I'm just standing up for my rights."

The policeman pointed to the swings. "A number of girls have been raped in this park," he said.

"So you think I'm the rapist?"

"Hand me your license and registration," the policeman demanded.

"I won't, because I've done nothing wrong."

When the policeman went back to his car, some of Jimmie's friends, who had arrived and witnessed the confrontation, pleaded with him to give the policeman what he wanted. Jimmie wouldn't budge from his position

In a few minutes, six more police cars arrived, surrounding Jimmie's vehicle. Again, his friends urged him to yield to the policeman's demand.

A black policeman was sent to persuade Jimmie to cooperate.

"But why should I? I'm not parked illegally. And you," he said, pointing at the black cop, "you know why the white policeman thinks I'm the rapist he's looking for. It's because of the color of my skin. You know that."

The black police officer refused to acknowledge Jimmie's assessment of the situation. "Look, brother," he said, "if you don't cooperate you're going to get yourself into a whole lot of trouble. So why don't you give me the license and registration. The man will look at it, give it back and leave you alone."

When Jimmie refused to hand over what was requested of him, two white policemen pulled him out of his car, handcuffed him and drove to the nearest police precinct where he was locked up for a day.

Jimmie had to hire a lawyer to file a protest with the police chief over the way he was treated. About three months later, two police officers called on Jimmie at dawn with a weak, written apology.

Jimmie's wife asked him why the police decided to come by so early. "They're resorting to psychological terrorism to remind us who is really the boss," he said.

W hite people in America, especially white males, aren't under the kind of pressure that blacks experience every day of their lives. Though born in this country, and with ancestors who have lived here longer than most whites' ancestors, blacks are made to feel they don't really belong in the land of their birth, that they are a social obstruction to the development of their country.

The celebrated writer, Toni Morrison, a black woman and a Princeton University professor, got to the heart of the matter when she wrote:

"Deep within the word 'American' is its association with race. To identify someone as a South African is to say very little; we need the adjective 'white' or 'black' or 'colored' to make our meaning clear. In this country it is quite the reverse. American means white, and Africanist people struggle to make the term applicable to themselves with ethnicity and hyphen after hyphen after hyphen. Americans (whites) did not have a profligate, predatory nobility from which to wrest an identity of national virtue while continuing to covet aristocratic license and luxury."

Though blacks see the advantages that whites enjoy in America just by being white, most whites have never taken the time to acquaint themselves with those advantages. We have taken them for granted.

9
Second-Class Citizens

The wounds that black people have sustained by living in the United States of America are deep and have yet to heal, despite the federal government's late twentieth century rush to right the wrongs of the past.

The wounds consist of a lack of confidence, a lack of self-esteem, feelings of inferiority and self-hatred. You can't wish them away; no amount of money can make them disappear; and no medicine or surgical procedure has been devised that can heal them. This doesn't mean, however, that they can't be healed.

The wounds fester in many blacks, sapping their vitality, restraining their drive to succeed in society, dimming their view of the future, and forcing them to find "something" that can numb the incessant pain in their lives. This is not only true for those who live in America's inner-city slums; many middle-class blacks suffer the same symptoms. With some affluence, they are able to mask the wounds effectively, but deep down they know they haven't healed.

You would think that the wounds would have healed by now, considering the signing of the Emancipation Proclamation, the end of Jim Crowism, the U.S. Supreme Court's ruling that ended school segregation, and affirmative action policies. They exist because the disease of racism still exists in whites. The continuous encounter with their nemesis is a reminder of black people's powerlessness, their second-class status. And it need not be a face-to-face encounter. Every time they board an airplane, there are stares from the white passengers, which aggravates the wounds and serves as reminder of the black person's social status in America.

Every time they watch television news, they are reminded of who has the power, who is benefiting from the "American Dream" – and who is habitually identified as the criminal, drug pusher, school dropout and welfare recipient.

Generally, blacks from countries outside of the United States aren't wounded, or, if they are, their wounds aren't so deep as those of the African-Americans. The reasons for the difference? They have a healthy sense of their culture; they come from lands where the majority of people are black; and those who run their governments are dark-skinned. As a consequence there's no racism. No racism, no wounds!

When black men and women from the West Indies come to America to attend college or start a business, they, in the main, don't lack self-esteem, they aren't plagued by self-hatred, and because of that, they usually succeed in achieving their educational and business goals. This pattern has caused some resentment among African-Americans. The reaction from the West Indians is to snub the American blacks, and, in some instances, view them as inferiors.

Though that's an unfair judgment, it is a reality.

This attitude is unfair because it fails to take into account the fact that the West Indian's background is different than that of his African-American counterpart. For while there was slavery in the West Indies, the slaves always outnumbered the white plantation owners on the islands on which they lived. So, when slavery was outlawed, they won their freedom. In the United States, the slaves were always a distinct minority. Any rebellion on their part would end up being a suicidal foray. The blacks in the United States were trapped. Even when the slaves were released from bondage, they didn't win their freedom. After flirting with it for a few years during the Reconstruction, they were swept into the jaws of Jim Crowism – once again preoccupied with survival and finding ways of subduing the pain produced by the wounds. Only when their wounds are healed will American blacks be truly free. And that's dependent on whites becoming seriously involved in curing their infection.

In the West Indies, blacks take pride in their ancestors' ability to defy and defeat their captors, the Europeans. They overthrew the French government in Haiti and declared it an independent state. In

Jamaica, numerous escaped slaves, called Maroons, repulsed every British attempt to recapture them. In what is presently called Suriname, Dutch troops were unable to subdue hundreds of escaped slaves who settled in the interior, setting up villages patterned after the communities they were forced to leave in Africa.

Naturally, many African-Americans prefer not to talk about their wounds, especially in public. After all, obsessing on one's flaws that seem impossible to correct can plunge a person into a state of depression. Just as many whites have done, many blacks have resorted to denial as a means of preserving their sanity.

In 1989, I discovered that it is especially disturbing to blacks when whites focus on the wounds. It is interpreted as an invasion of their privacy. After a talk I had given on racial unity, a middle-aged black woman took me aside and whispered, "You know, Nathan, when you talk about our wounds, you are opening up a can of worms. I wish you wouldn't do it anymore. Life is difficult enough for us. Reminders of our wounds, something we are powerless to deal with, make life even more difficult."

I felt terrible. My first reaction was to castigate myself for being so insensitive. Maybe withholding some aspects of the truth is necessary, I thought, in order to prevent unnecessary pain for the people I was trying to work with in overcoming racism. For the next six months, I never talked about the wounds. And that wasn't easy, because deep down I felt the decision I had made was wrong.

At first, I tried to ignore the feeling. Recalling the pain on my friend's face would help me repress it. But I couldn't hide from the wounds that were displayed every day in the classroom of the college where I was teaching then. My black students tried hard to mask them. They employed a variety of facades: There was the "tough guy" image; the flaunting of one's material possessions (something they had learned from whites); and the one that did the most damage – giving the impression that everything was "cool," when deep down they knew that wasn't true; and pretending that everything was fine, creating bogus personal achievements that they forced themselves to believe. Flights of fantasy, I have learned, can provide flashes of joy for troubled people.

I guess it's nature's way of dulling the pain. But, in the long run, you pay a price for that kind of psychological self-manipulation. You drift further and further away from reality, which can cause serious mental health problems. Now, it wasn't a case of my wounded students not being aware of their drift. They opted to continue their drift because there were no reasonable alternatives. To confront wholeheartedly their true social and economic condition would, they feared, plunge them into permanent rage that could only lead to disaster for themselves and those associated with them. So they chose the slower course to psychological death.

Since I knew they were wounded, I felt that, as their teacher, I should help them heal. I knew also that by not addressing their wounds the black students' intellectual and emotional development was being stunted – their human rights being violated. These young men and women were members of my family. I believed that with all my heart and soul, and yet I couldn't help them. I found myself tied to a commitment not to discuss the wounds caused by racism in public. I sensed this wasn't right.

In time, I broke that commitment. A series of events and some profound recollections freed me to develop ways of healing those wounds that can psychologically cripple a human being. I suspect the conversation I had with the old one-armed man was a factor in changing my mind. That experience had been pressed into my consciousness. What the old man said as we parted, I will never forget: *"It is the truth that will eventually make Americans free."*

P retending there were no wounds was a lie. And I knew what could happen if a wound wasn't attended to. The wounds are real and deep and force their victims to resort to dangerous ways to compensate for what they do to themselves to lessen the pain. I had learned of black children locking themselves in the bathroom and applying bleach all over their bodies in order to lighten their skin; of black adults using special skin-lightening creams and costly and painful hair-straightening processes; I saw highly-educated black men unconsciously suck in their lips while in the presence of whites.

In my quest for ways to heal the wounds, I came across a telling psychological study done in the early 1950s by Drs. Mamie and Kenneth Clark – both prominent psychologists and African-Americans. They tested three- to seven-year-old black children in several American cities to determine how extensive the wounds were. They ushered them into a room with a display of black and white dolls. The children were told: Give me the doll you like best; give me the nice doll; give me the doll that looks bad; and give me the doll that is the nice color. The great majority of the children preferred the white dolls.

Nearly forty years later, after the African-American community had been exposed to many "Black is Beautiful" campaigns, the test was redone – with no change in the results. Constant exposure to positive advertising campaigns can't erase what is continuously reinforced unwittingly at home, in school and in society in general.

Learning from friends and colleagues I greatly respected that they have never healed their wounds was also a factor in breaking my vow never to talk about the wounds in public, especially amongst blacks. Outwardly, they didn't give the impression of being wounded. They have been successful in almost every way – with good jobs, seemingly good marriages and happy, healthy children.

Because I was so close to some of these friends, and they trusted me, they were willing to share with me some of their deepest feelings pertaining to race. And they weren't hesitant to reveal some of their painful experiences. They knew I was writing a book about racism, and they wanted to help in my effort to expose the core of the problem.

One woman, an educator who had traveled widely and lived in Africa for ten years, recognized her wounds. Discovering them was somewhat of a shock, for she mingled freely, and with some degree of self-assurance, wherever she lived and worked. Her marriage to a prominent white man seemed to make her acceptable in most quarters. She was so busy pursuing a successful career and running a secure and healthy home, she didn't have time to think about her wounds.

But she was wounded, all right. And that realization took place in the most unlikely place – in a duplicating center in Cambridge, Massachusetts. Wanting a perfect photocopy of an important report she and her husband had written, she took her manuscript to what she had heard was one of the best duplicating centers in Cambridge.

When she stepped into the center, she thought she was in the wrong place. All of the personnel, as well as the owner, were black. Her immediate impulse was to leave, because her gut feeling was, "These people are incapable of the kind of job I want done." It didn't matter that she was black, that as a college youth she was a member of a black power radical organization that preached black separatism.

Because the shop was in Cambridge – the site of Harvard University – she had assumed that white people would be operating it, people she would feel had the expertise to do what she wanted done. The woman didn't leave. She stood near the entranceway in sort of a trance for a few moments, stunned that she – a college-educated black woman – could feel that way toward blacks. And there was nothing she could do to overcome that feeling. In some ways, that sense of helplessness to rid oneself of something one knows is wrong is worse than the wound itself.

You can have a Ph.D. and hold an important public post and still be wounded. This became apparent when Dr. Franklyn Jenifer came to the college where I taught to bid farewell to the faculty and administration. He was retiring as chancellor of the Massachusetts Board of Regents of Higher Education to become president of his alma mater, Howard University, a predominantly black institution.

Dr. Jenifer spoke from the heart. He appealed to the professors to make a concerted effort to help students of color overcome their lack of self-esteem, their sense of inferiority. Using himself as an example, he demonstrated how the wounds affect a person.

He shared with us an incident that had occurred shortly before he came to our campus. A distinguished academic organization had asked him to address a conference it was holding in Philadelphia. When he and his party arrived at the airport, they were told that the major airlines weren't flying to Philadelphia because of inclement weather. Only a commuter airline, located in a different terminal, was flying. After about a fifteen-minute wait, the pilot showed up. Dr. Jenifer's immediate reaction was not to board the small propeller-driven plane, because the pilot was black. He wanted a white person in the driver's seat, especially since the weather was bad. He knew it was wrong to feel that way, but that feeling was real, and there was nothing he could do to overcome it. And it didn't matter that he was a Ph.D., a noted microbiologist and the head of the state colleges and universities in Massachusetts – he was unable to repress that feeling that had been a part of him ever since he was a child.

P erhaps the most tragic victims of racism are those who have convinced themselves that they aren't wounded, that they have successfully assimilated into mainstream America. I met someone like that in my travels. This man was so much in denial that it was painful talking to him about the race issue. On other matters, he was charming, perfectly rational. He was a prosperous lawyer, articulate and well-read. He was proud of his beautiful white wife and their four bright sons. His hospitality and generosity were well known.

Casual observers felt that this man had it all, that despite the color of his skin, he was able to rise above the minefields of racism that saturate the American landscape.

Yet, up close, I saw a man who was ready to explode. Any deep discussions of his personal experiences with racism, I was sure, would set him off. As a consequence, his approach to the issue was always academic, never personal. Because he knew my stand on racism, he avoided me. But one time, he found himself in a position where he couldn't avoid me. It was at a small meeting called by a human rights organization. Race relations was the topic.

Conspicuously diplomatic, he complimented me on the work I was doing. That was tough to take, because I was aware of his efforts to sabotage what I and others were doing to heal the disease and wounds of racism.

After I described the nature of our race relations work, he smiled and said, "Please do me a favor and switch your focus to race unity."

"But there's no need to switch, because we are already working for racial unity," I said.

"I'm sorry, but I fail to see how discussions on healing what you call the disease and wounds of racism, and explaining how racism came about in America, are promoting race unity."

After pausing a moment, he added with some passion, "Don't you realize that we are all one?"

"Yes, I'm aware of the reality of the oneness of humankind, but most people aren't. And one of the reasons they aren't aware is because of the disease and wounds of racism. Once they begin to heal they are able to recognize that reality, and in time, they become a force for unity. I have seen that happen in our Institutes for the Healing of Racism," I replied.

"Promoting unity among people who are suspicious of one another, who are afraid of one another, who harbor deeply-rooted feelings of superiority or inferiority will only end up frustrating those making the effort. And in time, they'll give up trying. You can't have unity if you're continually trying to hide your infection or wounds. Deep down you'll know it's phony. The effort on everyone's part must be genuine. The process of unity begins when you recognize your infection or wounds and become involved in healing them.

"What we're dealing with is a disease. To keep it from spreading, we need to know its origin and pathology. Only with that knowledge can we devise an antidote for racism."

Knowing that he liked to march in race unity parades, I said, "While sponsoring race unity parades and picnics are nice, they won't heal the wounds or remove the poison of racism in people's hearts. Parades and picnics are symbols, wishful thinking giving the appearance, for an hour or two, of being real. What's needed is for black and white to face the truth, to find a place where we can help each other heal. That will lead to the blending of hearts; and then we can celebrate in the form of parades and picnics, with our heads held high."

Trying hard to mask his anger, he sat back and said, "I just don't see any value in ripping away the scabs of the past."

I didn't respond. Though part of me wanted to shake him and tell him what other blacks thought of him, I restrained myself. He hadn't fooled them. To many of them, he was an "Oreo," someone black on the outside and white on the inside, like the cookie. They sensed that he was basically ashamed of being black.

By contrast, I met a young black man whose honesty and calm in the face of adversity was an inspiration to me. I learned a great deal from him just by observing how he lived life. He had a healthy understanding of who he was, of his heritage and the realities pertaining to race relations in society. He knew that the social situation for blacks was far from perfect. There were indignities suffered daily by blacks who had to deal with whites regularly. And he was no exception. At one time he would have reacted angrily to slights by whites. But no longer.

While interviewing him for a television documentary, I gained an understanding of his approach to racist acts directed at him. He told me of an incident that had occurred that day:

He made his purchases at a supermarket, he said, and, after loading them into his car, was pushing his grocery cart back toward the store. At this point, he said, an elderly white woman called to him, "You don't have to collect the basket, because I'm going inside to shop."

It was pretty clear to him, my friend said, that, because he was black and dressed in casual clothes, the woman, though pleasant, had made the automatic assumption that he was an employee, assigned to round up grocery carts in the parking lot. He handed over the cart to the woman, without comment.

"Now, I know she meant no harm, nor did she harbor any ill will toward me. What she said was perfectly natural for her," my friend told me.

He added, however, "I must admit that it hurt, especially on that day. Only two hours earlier I had successfully defended my master's thesis in engineering at the University of Massachusetts."

When I asked him why that incident didn't anger him, he said, "At one time I would have been angry, but when I learned that by being human I was inherently a noble being, I could only respond to someone in a noble fashion.

"My hope is that more people will gain that perspective, for it has a way of dissolving hate and fear in human hearts."

After the TV interview, and while the crew was putting away the gear, I asked the young man what caused his switch in attitude.

"I came across a passage in the Bahá'í writings that intrigued me – and challenged me to discover what it claimed I and every other human being on this planet possess," he said.

"What was the passage?" I asked.

He recited it by heart:

"O Son of Spirit!

"I created thee rich, why dost thou bring thyself down to poverty? Noble I made thee, wherewith dost thou abase thyself? Out of the essence of knowledge I gave thee being, why seekest thou enlightenment from anyone beside Me? Out of the clay of love I moulded thee, how dost thou busy thyself with another? Turn thy sight unto thyself, that thou mayest find Me standing within thee, mighty, powerful and self- subsisting."

10
Marked For Failure

Most of us have been brought up to believe that, through education, societal ills like race prejudice can be cured. After all, with knowledge we can overcome ignorance, as the saying goes. And isn't prejudice an emotional commitment to ignorance?

Unfortunately, our schools, which have been around for a long time, have done little to eliminate racism in our communities. In fact, because of the way they are structured and staffed, they, until this day, reinforce existing racial attitudes. It isn't something that is being done consciously. The principals and teachers aren't bigots. Many of them do their jobs well; they are dedicated educators.

But since most of them are white, and have been brought up in America, they unknowingly have been exposed to the virus of racism and infected. This doesn't make them evil people. They are sick and don't know it. They unwittingly aggravate the wounds of the students of color in their classes. How? By what they say and do, and the kinds of textbooks they use. It is obvious that they aren't aware of the black students' wounds. If they were, they would be more careful with what they say and do in the classroom, and devise a curriculum that would help heal the wounds.

But that's not happening in most of America's independent, parochial and public schools. It is one of the major reasons why many black students, in particular, have difficulty in school. For them, the classroom is an arena of defeat, a factory of failure. They don't want to be there, because it revives their feelings of inferiority and self-hatred. In order to combat those destructive feelings, they resort to education-bashing, often belittling any of their friends who try to excel academically.

What I discovered by teaching courses in television techniques at an urban community college populated by many black and Latino students is that their anti-education attitude changes to love for education when they experience some academic success – and respect. Their primary aim for attending my program was to learn an employable skill that would provide them with respectable jobs.

Aware of their wounds, I created a teaching approach and curriculum to build up their self-esteem. As a consequence, most of the black students went on to earn their bachelor's and master's degrees. Some earned doctorates.

Because of bad experiences in one of the "best" public school systems in New England, George didn't want to have anything to do with education after dropping out of high school. His mother, a Ph.D. and a successful educational administrator, knew what his teachers didn't know – that her son was bright. Throughout his junior and high school years, he had been kept out of the college preparatory track, and was urged by counselors to pursue a trade like auto mechanics or plumbing. He rebelled, because he couldn't accept the school system's diagnosis. Deep down, he knew he could be a good film maker, or a journalist. He left high school because he felt the tracking system had branded him a slow learner, and he knew he wasn't; every time he tried to explain how he felt, he would become angry, which would usually lead to a suspension from school. His decision to drop out wasn't contested by any of the teachers or administrators, because they thought they were getting rid of a trouble-maker.

Aware of what we were doing at Springfield Technical Community College, George's mother asked if I would try to persuade her son to enter our program. I contacted him, and her wish was fulfilled.

George graduated with honors, had been elected vice president of the Student Senate, and had been selected by his peers to anchor the campus TV newscast. He went on to a four-year college, where he excelled, and is on his way to achieving his professional goal.

Now, George was lucky. And he knows it. For most other black students who were driven out of the public school system never return to school. Whatever career dreams they had as youngsters have been dashed. They usually end up becoming a part of the unskilled labor force – or in trouble with the law.

Mark's career dream had been dashed. Our only meeting was at a gathering organized to interview black and Latino students concerning the racism reported by them at the high school they attended. Mark was the first one to speak. At his previous school in Cleveland, which was predominantly black, he was an "A" student. His strongest subjects were mathematics and science. He dreamed of becoming an electrical engineer. His voice began to quiver as he related what it was like being at his new school, which was predominantly white:

"I was the only black in the class. Some students would say hello, but it was a hollow greeting. We never engaged in any meaningful discussions. They were always in a rush to meet their friends. And the teachers rarely called on me in class, even though I knew the answers. It was as if they didn't think I knew the answers, or they were afraid I would embarrass myself by making a foolish remark. I felt alone and invisible. It got so bad that, when I would enter the classroom, I felt isolated, worthless, dirty. I couldn't wait until the period-ending bell would ring. I was so uptight I couldn't concentrate. I wondered if I was a misfit.

"Then my grades started to fall, and I was removed from the college prep track. There was no way I was going to be an electrical engineer."

At that moment Mark started to cry. His dream had been dashed. His teachers, who I'm sure meant well, didn't realize that they had psychologically murdered the young man. They went home each afternoon unaware of Mark's agony. As I gazed at the weeping youngster, I wondered about the countless other black students in America who have had similar experiences.

There are psychological and biological reasons why students like Mark do poorly in school. While in Hawaii, I learned of the work of Dr. Kenneth Yamamoto, a highly respected human developmentalist. Months later, during a telephone conversation, he shared with me his knowledge of what happens to a student who feels insecure, suffers from feelings of inferiority, and enters a classroom. The student's cerebral cortex, which is the seat of thought, shuts down. His medulla oblongata, which is at the base of the brain and controls emotions, takes over. The student is seized by survival emotions. He either wants to fight or flee. Those who end up fighting generally are categorized as behavior problems, and often are shunted off to special classes for the emotionally impaired. Some may be given tranquilizers, which dull their thinking processes. Often the teacher who is quick to label a student doesn't know why the child is angry. Her decision is based on fear, which is a manifestation of her unconscious race prejudice. She doesn't know that the student's anger is actually a protest at being unfairly judged by an institution that's too powerful for him to contest. He senses that he's viewed as a dummy and is being sentenced to special classes for dummies for the rest of his school days. As for those students who want to flee, they either drop out of school or drop out psychologically, attending classes only because their parents insist that they do – and end up graduating as functional illiterates.

Harry Morgan noted in an article titled "How Schools Fail Black Children," that most black children suffer from what he calls the "third grade syndrome."

"When blacks enter first grade the stories they create express positive feelings about themselves in the schooling situation," he says, "but by the second grade students' stories express negative imagery of the teacher and school environment; and by the fifth grade the overall feeling expressed by students is that of cynicism. In other words, upon entering schools in primary grades, black children possess enthusiasm and eager interest, however, by fifth grade the liveliness and interest are gone, replaced by passivity and apathy. Primary grades presented a more nurturing environment than intermediate or upper grades. In early childhood education much of the activity is child-teacher centered and child-child interactive. In primary grades, blacks progress and thrive at the same rate as their white counterparts until the third grade syndrome. I found after the third grade, the achievement rate of blacks began a downward spiral which tended to continue in the child's academic career. The classroom environment was transformed from a socially interactive style to a competitive, individualistic, and minimally socially interactive style of learning."

I am convinced that black students' disenchantment with education does not mean that they don't want to be educated. It is the racism they often confront in the classroom that they can't abide. For most, it starts during the early grades of elementary school. Social psychologist Claude M. Steele, himself black, claims that because of the way schools are set up in most communities, African-American children are doomed to do poorly. They are plagued by two fears: the fear of being devalued and the fear of exposing their lack of ability.

The educational environment is a factor. Their teachers and principals are usually white, which is interpreted by the black children as evidence that whites possess the power, and are superior to blacks. And this impression is reinforced when the school's janitors and cafeteria staff are primarily black. The students rarely complain. They simply observe, and the message is registered.

Textbooks often contribute to the fostering of racism in schools. Though publishers aren't aware of it, what they produce irritates and deepens the wounds of black students. What escapes the publisher escapes the teacher as well – but not the black child and his or her parents.

Nine-year-old Yolanda, for example, felt that her social studies textbook's view that blacks won equal status with whites when the Civil War ended was incorrect. She knew better, because of the things her parents and relatives would share with each other concerning racism. What she would see on television and read in magazines and newspapers corroborated her parents' views and her personal feelings. The child knew in her heart that blacks weren't treated as equals with whites.

Yet, neither she nor her parents complained to the teacher. In fact, in her social studies exam Yolanda put down the textbook's version of when blacks won equal status with whites – even though she didn't believe it. She did it because she wanted to do what the teacher thought was right.

But even textbooks that mention the Civil Rights Movement of the 1960s – and may even feature a picture of Dr. Martin Luther King, Jr. – often foster racism. Again, the publishers are unaware of what they have done. In fact, they may be proud of devoting twenty pages to the contributions of "minorities" in the development of the United States of America. What they neglect to consider, however, is the overall message the book conveys to the students, black and white. In one New England school noted for its progressive social outlook, the eighth-graders were using a history textbook that devoted twenty-five pages to minority contributions, and the remaining 325 pages to the exploits and achievements of the whites. You don't have to be a genius to figure out who are the more important people, the ones with the power. The students can count. The group that receives 325 pages of coverage has to be superior to others, which, combined, only receive twenty-five. Unfortunately, this subtle racist message communicated by the textbook isn't noticed by the teacher. The black parent's assessment of the coverage discrepancy is that the publisher is either casting crumbs to the students of color, or trying to placate the minorities in the community.

The greatest offenders are the teachers and administrators. I know that this view will be challenged. I will be accused of making an unfair sweeping indictment of professionals who are trying to do the best job possible under difficult conditions.

It isn't their sense of dedication that I question, or their teaching ability. Nor am I finding fault with their character. Most of them, I'm sure, are good people who want to do the right thing in the classroom.

The problem is that they are unaware of the damage they are doing, because they are unaware of the fact that they are infected by the disease of racism. Though it is something they didn't choose, they picked up the infection just by being American whites. Usually when confronted with that fact, a teacher recoils in anger, becomes defensive. Getting the teacher to deal with the infection while in that state of mind is almost impossible.

It is understood by everyone that black students won't be exposed to blatant racist attacks from teachers. Racist graffiti will be condemned by the administration and faculty; so will any white student's verbal abuse of a black student. And Black History Month will be celebrated; every student will write essays about Martin Luther King, Jr. in commemoration of his birthday. Yet, it is the little things that teachers say or do, or don't say or do, that deepens the wounds of black children on a regular basis.

Carlos' mother has done a good job in acquainting him with his culture. Unlike many black youngsters attending predominantly white schools, Carlos will address any racial slight, be it subtle or overt. As a seventh-grader, he knew that he had been branded a troublemaker by the school authorities. Most teachers in his presence anticipated trouble. Though he didn't belong in a special education class, he had been placed in one, because that's where trouble-makers are quarantined.

The more Carlos resisted the racism in class, the more difficulty he encountered from teachers and school officials. One incident in particular, involving Carlos, caught the attention of the news media. Almost immediately, a rash of denial broke out in the community. Men and women – many of them avowed liberals – proclaimed that Carlos' charge couldn't be true, for their town was one of the most socially enlightened towns in America.

But Carlos was telling the truth. I know, because as a member of the NAACP's local education committee, I had been asked by the executive council to investigate Carlos' claim. Not only was the young man's charge true, but I was exposed to the school system's clumsy attempt to cover up the incident. This was done by shifting the blame to Carlos. News reporters were told that the young man was incorrigible in class; that he was practically a juvenile delinquent. (Actually, Carlos had a sweet nature and an outgoing personality that would bubble up into enthusiasm when he liked something or someone.)

To get the school's side of the story, I called on the junior high school's acting director of curriculum and staff development. (The principal refused to talk to me, and until this day refuses to even acknowledge my greetings.)

The acting director was a pleasant man, who had been in the school system many years. Because he was proud of the system and his record in it, I sensed that he viewed me as a prospective enemy who was bent on defaming something that was good. He became an ardent defender:

"I know about Carlos' charge," he said, "but first it's important to put everything into perspective. You must consider the source of the charge. The boy has repeatedly gotten into trouble. Frankly, he's a behavioral problem."

"I'm aware that he has had run-ins with his teachers, that he's no angel," I said. "But that's not the point.

"Is it true that his teacher refused to allow him to do a profile of Dr. George Washington Carver instead of the other scientists listed in his textbook, who were all white?"

"Mr. Rutstein," he said, "you don't have the facts straight."

"Well, straighten me out – that's why I'm here, to get your side of the story."

"You see, Carlos never mentioned Dr. George Washington Carver. What he said was, 'I want to do a biography of the black man who invented peanut butter.'"

Flabbergasted, I said, "I want to make two points. The first is important, but the second one is more important.

"First, I think that anyone who is teaching junior high school social studies should be able to make the connection between peanut butter and its inventor, Dr. Carver.

"Second, I think Carlos, like other black students, wants a learning experience that's related to his cultural heritage. And our

106

teachers should understand why it's important that they provide those opportunities for black students.

"By rejecting Carlos' request, the teacher not only rejected the youngster's wish, she devalued the contributions of a black scientist, thus reinforcing the prevailing national notion that whites are inherently superior to blacks, that blacks don't really count. Every time that happens to a person like Carlos, his impression of himself is diminished."

"But you don't understand," the acting director protested. "We are committed to multiculturalism."

"Look," he said, holding up a chart. "Next Monday we begin our celebration of Diversity Week. We have more than thirty events our students can choose from. There's Cambodian cuisine, the traditional Japanese tea ceremony, Russian folk songs, Native American artifacts – including a real teepee, a lecture on African-American writers."

He pointed with pride to the last box on the chart, and said, "We even got a black rock'n'roll group to come up from the city to do a concert. It will be held in our gymnasium."

All I could say was, "That's nice." To say what I wanted to say would have been a waste of time and effort. He wasn't ready to hear how I really felt about the school's multicultural endeavor. It was another Band-Aid; another attempt to placate the growing number of people of color in town; and a way of silencing the system's critics – like the local branch of the NAACP. What was needed was a way for the teachers to address their infection, become aware of the wounds of students of color, and devise ways of healing those wounds.

The vast majority of teachers in that school had no idea of the pain endured by Carlos and his mother. They had no idea of what the young man was calling for every time he confronted his teachers. They lacked the intuition and sensitivity to sense Carlos' needs, because they were unaware of his wounds. The teachers left school each day satisfied with their classroom efforts, hoping the administration would find some way to get rid of troublemakers like Carlos.

About two months after the peanut butter incident, an attempt was made to place Carlos in a special school the system created to warehouse the undesirable boys and girls in town who refused to become dropouts.

Carlos' mother – with the help of the NAACP – thwarted the attempt. Carlos, meanwhile, continues to struggle in a school that doesn't want him ... and he knows it.

Even schools that stress moral education aren't free of racism. Dolores found that out, much to her regret. When the African-American single parent of two daughters moved to New Haven to attend Yale University's graduate school, she tried to find the right school for her children. After carefully checking the elementary school situation, she opted to send her two daughters to what was considered the best Catholic school in the city. Though not a Catholic, Dolores wanted her children's learning experience to include moral training. She was also impressed with the school's curriculum; multiculturalism was emphasized in each grade. The principal was another reason Dolores decided to send her daughter to the parochial school. The nun had a loving and caring spirit. To pay her girl's tuition, Dolores worked weekends as a registered nurse at a local hospital. And she could count on her mother in Atlanta to help out financially. Both women were willing to make sacrifices in order to assure the children received the best education.

About a month into the first semester, Dolores' ten-year-old daughter came home with what on the surface seemed like a reasonable assignment. To the young mother, it was far from reasonable – it was a serious warning sign. Frankly, she expected the teacher to be more sensitive to the needs of black children. Dolores first met the teacher during orientation week, and was favorably impressed. In many ways she was like the principal – loving and caring. And from the decorations in her classroom, the teacher seemed innovative and well organized. Dolores remembered thinking at the time: "How I wish I'd had the opportunity to study in a classroom like this."

After clearing the dishes from the dinner table, Dolores' eldest daughter went to her mother for homework help. "Mommy," she said, "my teacher wants all of us to write a profile of the country our ancestors came from."

Dolores was appalled. Africa was a huge continent with more than forty nations. She had no idea where her ancestors lived before they were forced to come to America as slaves.

"Mom," the child complained, "why are you taking so long?"

"Just thinking."

"About what?"

At that point Dolores remembered that she knew who had fathered her great-grandmother. He was a white man, a Georgia state senator whose ancestral roots were in Ireland. The man had raped her great-great-grandmother.

"Honey," Dolores said, "I know that most of our ancestors came from Africa, but I don't know from what country. But I'm sure of where your great-great-great-grandfather came from – Ireland."

"So I'll do the profile on Ireland," the child said.

"That's okay."

After the assignment was handed in, Dolores wrote the teacher a letter, explaining why that particular assignment was inappropriate for black fifth-graders. She also explained the circumstances that led her child to do a profile on Ireland.

In responding to Dolores' letter, the teacher defended the issuance of the assignment in question: "In doing the assignment the student becomes acquainted with his or her ancestral roots and develops pride in their heritage; and when the profiles are read in class all of the students develop an appreciation of each other's cultures, thus creating a spirit of tolerance in class."

Frank, the other black child in the class, didn't fare as well as Dolores' child. No one wrote a letter on his behalf.

When he told his teacher that his mother didn't know what country his ancestors came from, she suggested he ask his grandmother. When she didn't know, Frank found himself in a dilemma. He didn't want to tell his teacher what his grandmother had told him, because he didn't want to give the impression that his family was made up of a bunch of dummies. Yet, he had to produce a profile.

Frank decided on a compromise, and chose to do one on China.

His reasons: The Chinese weren't white, and he wanted to be associated with a famous culture. He worked hard on the assignment.

When the students were asked for volunteers to read their profiles, Frank's hand shot up. As he read with great pride, students began to giggle. In a few minutes the giggling exploded into side-splitting laughter. Even the teacher laughed.

Only Frank didn't laugh – his little black hands curled into fists as he fought back tears.

Black students' poor performance in school, I am convinced, has nothing to do with lack of intelligence. It has to do with their dread of being devalued and their fear of lacking ability in the classroom. These fears are manifested the day they start school and are reinforced in grade after grade, creating a mounting pressure that drives them to either give up trying or drop out. Suffering that kind of defeat deepens their wounds and intensifies their anger and bitterness.

Obviously, the key to overcoming those fears is having teachers understand why those fears exist, and how they thwart intellectual development – and, above all, how to make black students feel valued. Without knowledge of the former, the latter is unattainable.

11
Lost Opportunities

I'm not so naive as to believe that schools and other community institutions will automatically embrace what I propose. There will be resistance even from individuals and institutions that espouse progressive ideals.

Of course, that saddens me, especially when women and men want to do the right thing and like what you offer, but refuse to embrace it for fear of alienating a certain constituency.

An elderly member of an Institute for the Healing of Racism in Florida ran into such a person: "He was a minister of an all-white church. But I didn't meet him there. It was at the community college where he was teaching a comparative religion course. The preacher seemed so progressive and sympathetic to human rights causes. When I told him about the formation of an Institute in town, he urged everyone in our class to join. But when I approached him after class, and asked him to make a similar appeal to his congregation, he leaned toward me and whispered, 'If I did that I would lose my job.' "

Then there are officials who oppose a new idea, not on philosophical grounds, but because it threatens their professional security. To make sure the threat never materializes, they'll stoop to scare tactics.

When the minister of an all-black church in Delaware heard that some of his parishioners had joined the Institute for the Healing of Racism, he demanded that they quit immediately, claiming that working with Bahá'ís was a sure way to go to hell. Sadly, the pastor's call was heeded.

Though racism has been around for a long time and we think about it from time to time, we rarely discuss it, especially in mixed company. Mainly because it is such a volatile issue; and, there's always the chance of having to face a part of ourselves that we've been afraid to confront, because we've tried hard to convince others that it doesn't exist.

For most blacks and whites, interracial discussion evokes emotions that are difficult to control. Hence, the tendency among society's public and private agencies is to avoid the subject as long as possible. When they are forced to deal with it, the least painful path to a solution is taken, which invariably produces unsatisfactory results. Oh, the effort may quiet the protesters for a while, but the centuries-old problem, racism, continues to smolder beneath the surface of the community, flaring up from time to time.

Sadly, more thought and time are devoted to developing effective means of avoiding the central issue than confronting it with a commitment to overcoming it. As long as the present strategy is capable of buying time, the agencies will continue to employ it. The fear of facing the central issue is so deeply rooted that even riots stimulated by racial distress, like those in Watts and South Central Los Angeles, are unable to persuade the agencies to forego their reliance on superficial solutions for restoring order and relative calm. Unfortunately, the longer the central issue is avoided, the more difficult it will be to deal with it. For fear grows when not overcome. And the greater the fear, the greater the struggle will be to solve the central issue. But one thing is certain: Eventually it will have to be addressed. Like death, it is just a matter of time before it is dealt with.

It isn't always a matter of ignorance that prevents the agency leadership from dealing with the central issue. Deep down they're aware of the problem and their reluctance to face it. Lacking the certitude and courage to tackle it, they resort to aspirin and Band-Aid measures in dealing with racism issues, hoping that enough time will pass between incidents so that someone else will have to deal with it. Over the years, "passing the buck" has become a sophisticated practice in America.

In the past two years, I watched a superintendent of schools try to pass the buck, knowing full well that doing the safe thing was the wrong thing to do. It was a decision that I suspect tormented him.

He came to his job in Massachusetts heralded as the savior of a deteriorating school system, and he had reason to be proud of his vision of reform. It was well thought-out and comprehensive, providing solutions to the system's problem areas. All but one. And that was racism, which had never been identified by the school board as a problem. After two months on the job, he discovered that the system he had been asked to save was packaged in denial. It wasn't something that he imagined. Being a member of a minority ethnic group, he had considerable experience with spotting and dealing with racism.

Politically, he knew it would be a mistake to reveal to the public what he had discovered. He needed someone else, someone with influence in the city to join him in declaring that racism existed in the school system. No one of influence was willing to make a joint proclamation.

My first meeting with the superintendent was made possible through a friend of mine – a member of the school board. The friend had sent him a copy of a position paper I had helped author, "Healing Racism: Education's Role."

The first thing the superintendent said when we met was, "Thanks for the paper. It was a godsend, for it is what we need. Racism in this city is widespread, affecting everyone in our schools." He pointed to a stack of papers on his desk and said, "I've made over a hundred copies of your paper, and every principal will get a copy."

I was impressed with his attitude and the desire to get things done immediately. He suggested starting a pilot project in the city's largest middle school.

In a few weeks a project was started. The teachers involved in it were enthusiastic about what they had volunteered to do. The growth they noticed in themselves and their students was the major

113

source of their enthusiasm. But there were disappointments. The biggest one was not getting follow-up support from the superintendent. He never encouraged the participants, or inquired about the project's progress. In time, it fizzled.

Our second meeting had to do with a documentary I was doing on racism in the city. In the interview, he philosophized, carefully avoiding what he had discovered within his own system. He made sure to say all of the right things. After the camera was shut down, he revealed his latest strategy in ridding the system of racism. He was going to organize the city's clergy – black and white – to help wipe out racism in the classroom. He never mentioned the earlier pilot project. The superintendent's plan was never implemented.

An incident subsequently occurred which should have – but didn't – make it easier for the superintendent to take some positive steps toward curing the disease of racism he knew was present in his big-city school system.

An English teacher in one of the system's high schools wrote a letter, which she believed was confidential, to a member of the school committee in a neighboring community. The smaller, suburban community was considering the admission to its own schools of some students from the core city, where the teacher was employed, and was looking for advice. The letter described the city's predominantly black and Hispanic student population as promiscuous, ridden with sexually transmitted diseases, and violent. It was a bomb – waiting to explode.

And explode it did, when, instead of remaining private as intended, the letter was made part of the committee's public records. It also made headlines, generated widespread denunciations in political, religious and minority circles – with the superintendent wholeheartedly joining in – and led to the teacher's resignation.

A close friend of mine, a highly-respected public relations figure in the state, concluded it was time – with this example so painfully available – to bring the various agencies in the city together to wage war on racism. Aware of what I was doing, he suggested to certain leaders in the city that they hear what my associates and I had done in other cities.

The meeting was held at the superintendent's office. In attendance were a representative of the school board, the executive director of the Council of Churches, the superintendent, a local leading attorney and social activist, my friend and I.

When I shared what we were able to do and how we did it, the enthusiastic response from the clergywoman and school board member encouraged the superintendent to add his support. In his remarks, he pointed out with some pride that he was aware of our race unity plan and had started implementing it through a pilot project in one of the schools.

He went on to say that he would like me to address all of the system's teachers, adding, "The sooner the better. How about in two weeks?"

A high school auditorium was suggested as the meeting place. Everyone approved of the superintendent's idea.

It was heartening to see the beleaguered superintendent doing something he believed in. He said, time and time again, how grateful he was for meeting that day; how appreciative he was of our support; and that he would do all he could to get our plan implemented throughout the system. All of us left thinking that a brilliant start had been made in overcoming racism in the city.

But a week later, we noticed that the superintendent's fire was fading fast. His public relations director had advised against adopting our plan, and my address to the teachers was postponed indefinitely.

To try to save the situation, my public relations friend arranged a meeting between me, the superintendent, the teacher's union president and a school board member who had expressed interest in our plan.

From the start, it appeared hopeless. The superintendent wasn't paying attention to what was being said, and seemed distracted, unable to keep his mind on the subject. The teachers' union president was doing most of the speaking. The fast-talking, slim, gray-haired unionist never smiled. It was obvious that she knew how to wield power, something the superintendent respected.

After trying to convince us of her dedication to civil rights by

115

pointing out how many freedom marches she participated in in the 1960s, and that some of her closest friends were university Afro-American studies department professors, she explained why she was opposed to my speaking to the teachers. "There are only eight more weeks 'til the end of the academic year, and our teachers are tired," she said. "They can't take another thing. I have never seen such a desire among teachers to leave the classroom. I don't think they would be interested."

Listening to her was a test that I almost failed. When she said the teachers were too tired to take on something new, I wanted to cry out, "Look here, sister! What about the years of neglect and discrimination that black and Latino children have been exposed to in our schools? Don't you think our teachers should take the time to find ways to heal the black and Latino children's wounds? To end the psychological crippling that goes on in our classrooms? Don't you think teachers should be aware of how they can play a role in curing the cancer of racism?"

I didn't try to dissuade her, because I knew that nothing I would say could change her mind. She enjoyed winning battles.

Of course, the superintendent was supportive of her position. To please her, he added what he felt she believed. "Nathan, the teachers wouldn't buy your approach, because you might come off as some sort of savior," he said.

I was too hurt to try to defend myself. It was my friend who came to my rescue.

"How can you say that when you haven't heard the man's talk," he said, looking at the superintendent with an incredulous smile. "I've heard him. I wouldn't be here today if I didn't feel that what he has to say will make an important difference. I went to the University of Vermont to hear him speak, and I saw the effect he had on the audience and what it led to – the formation of an Institute for the Healing of Racism."

Obviously impressed by what my friend had to say, the superintendent apologized to me and came up with a compromise: "What about having Nathan speak to the principals, the same time and place ... but closed to the press?" He turned to the union president and asked, "What do you think?"

"It's okay with me," she said.

I left the superintendent's office, devoid of any desire to work with the school system. The obstacles to getting done what had to be done seemed overwhelming. With vacillating leadership, it seemed impossible to mobilize the teachers and administrators to wage a war against racism in the classroom.

In a way I was relieved when I was told several days later that the talk to the principals had been canceled because, according to the superintendent, there was a lack of interest.

The only thing that bothered me was that the students would continue to function in an unhealthy social climate, a climate that was reinforcing the existing prejudices in the schools. This, despite attempts at multiculturalism and some cultural sensitivity training for the teachers – exercises installed to enhance the system's image rather than produce a student body and faculty free of racial prejudice.

The superintendent's actions didn't anger me, for I realized that, in reality, his title wasn't indicative of the power most people felt it signified. He wasn't free to carry out what his heart told him was right. There were certain practical and political considerations that took precedence. Warring with the teachers' union would destroy whatever harmony existed in the system. I believe it was with reluctance that he opted for an approach that would preserve the status quo. Knowing that he had the backing of the school board and the union was comforting, because it helped to solidify his job.

As for the union president? I feel no ill will toward her, because I'm sure she did what she thought was best for the union membership. Her narrow focus was not born out of an ingrained selfishness, for she had given a lot of her time, energy and money to human rights causes. As a social activist, she had fought the civil rights battle in the sixties, and had scars to prove it. Because racism still exists after all that was done to eradicate it in the sixties and seventies, I feel she believes that it is impossible to get rid of; and having me speak to the teachers would be a waste of everyone's time.

The rejection didn't discourage me from doing what I feel has to be done. There were other fields to plough. I am sure that, along the way, some educators will arise, putting principle ahead of every-thing else, and adopt our plan that, if administered properly, could be a vaccine against the disease of racism.

It's understandable why even people of good will are suspicious of what we propose. After all, there is the human tendency to resist change, even the changing of ways and beliefs that most of us agree require change. What is usually resisted is a proposed solution that seems foreign – like teaching the principle of the oneness of human-kind. It is feared because acceptance could end an emotional commit-ment to a lifelong belief. It doesn't matter that science recognizes all people, regardless of geographical location or skin color, as members of one family. Abandoning an old belief is viewed by many people as an intrusion of their "comfort zone."

All sorts of excuses are raised to discredit a foreign proposed solution, especially if it's untried. The Institute for the Healing of Racism in one Southern city ran into that kind of opposition when it tried to persuade the city's school system to teach the oneness of humankind in the classroom.

Three members of the Institute were grilled by a panel of educa-tional experts. The interrogation began with a demand to explain the origin and purpose of the Institute.

"How is it financed?" asked one of the panelists.

When the three Institute members laughed, one of the experts asked, "What's so funny?"

"Sir," said Joan, one of the Institute's members, "we found the question funny, because we are as poor as church mice. We have no budget. Whatever money we use to print flyers, mail letters and make phone calls comes out of our personal budgets."

"Aren't you receiving funding from your national organiza-tion?"

"Sir, we have no national organization," she replied.

"I find that hard to believe," said the only woman on the panel.

"It's true," said Joan, feeling pressured. "We dig into our own pockets."

The skeptical college professor on the panel said sarcastically, "I suppose you dig into your pockets because of your desire to serve your fellow man."

"That's true," said Joan. "We do what we're doing because we want to do something to help heal the disease of racism and unite the human family. By teaching the oneness of humankind in school, we feel, strides will be made to eradicate racism and bring us together."

The professor shook his head in disbelief.

"Intellectuals won't buy your theory," he said.

"It is not a theory, it's a fundamental truth," said Joan.

"Prove it to me!"

"Have you read our position paper – 'Healing Racism: Education's Role'?"

"I've skimmed through it," said the professor, skeptically.

"The paper cites scientific proof, and we could provide more evidence."

Anita, one of the other Institute members, couldn't contain herself. "Professor, intellectuals don't have all of the answers," she said.

"I didn't say we do."

"I'm sure you are aware," said Anita, "that in the Dark Ages it was intellectuals who tried to debunk the idea that our planet was round, employing logic and mathematics to prove that the Earth was flat and the center of the universe."

The director of the school system's curriculum center entered the fray.

"To be blunt, I'm afraid to adopt your plan, because it could lead to a form of brainwashing of our students ... you know, mind control."

"I don't understand," countered Joan, showing signs of bewilderment. "How could learning about something that science recognizes as truth be construed as brainwashing?"

"Well, because I, for one, sense that you have a hidden agenda, that you are using your position paper as a wedge to indoctrinate our students with the teachings of your faith," the director said.

"As a Christian, I believe that all humans are God's children. Do you disagree?" asked Joan.

"No, but I thought you were a Bahá'í"

"I'm the Bahá'í in this group," said Anita. "It's true that a group of Bahá'ís came up with the concept of the Institute for the Healing of Racism and wrote the position paper. But believe me, what we created was not a proselytizing ploy. What was conceived was born out of a sincere desire to serve the community at large, to try to heal what is destroying our nation. We envisioned people of all religions working together in this endeavor, and, by God, we have been able to do that.

"You can rest assured that there is no secret command post that is constantly monitoring and directing our operation.

"We were functioning before the National Bahá'í Center became aware of our existence. And for your information, the center never blessed our social enterprise or officially sanctioned it."

Two days later Joan received a phone call from one of the panel members, saying that the panel wasn't ready to endorse the Institute's proposal.

12
More Than Multiculturalism

The growing number of racial flare-ups in schools has forced educators to look for quick solutions and reliable preventive measures. Some school districts are in a panic.

Unfortunately, much of their search is focused on finding a suitable anti-racism curriculum for students, when, in fact, the primary focus should be on the teachers. For it is the instructor who sets the tone and tempo of a class. If the teacher isn't committed to the cause of eradicating racism or isn't aware of the nature of the problem, then a good anti-racism curriculum won't be enthusiastically carried out, and the desired classroom result won't be achieved. And there's always a good chance that a teacher who hasn't dealt with his own infection will unwittingly exhibit an attitude and behavior that contradicts what is being taught in a race relations class. One- or two-day diversity appreciation workshops every year may give the impression that some good is being done, but they won't heal the teacher's infection.

Ideally, every school should maintain an ongoing workshop that's designed to heal the infection and wounds of racism that afflict the faculty, administrators and the rest of the staff. The workshop should be held on a regular basis throughout the academic year, preferably after school. Twice a month, even once a month, would suffice. What's important is regularity. To assure universal participation, a stipend should be given to all of the participants.

The principal should participate, and not only make one or two appearances. Symbolic appearances are nice, but what helps to highlight the seriousness of the institutional racism-purging exercise is the leadership's wholehearted involvement. Such action usually inspires hesitant teachers to become involved.

Even if the principal is indifferent, and the program starts with only a few dedicated teachers, it will grow in size and appeal when its participants remain patient, persistent and united in purpose. As it makes progress, more of the timid teachers will join, and the school's skeptics will be less critical, some of them becoming open-minded, even supportive. When the skeptics begin to become involved, the teachers who are straddling the fence will follow. Perceived miracles have a way of stimulating action.

In time, the ongoing workshop could take on school problems that stem from racial misunderstandings among students and teachers. It would function as an in-house combination court and sensitivity training center.

This is the Institute for the Healing of Racism, already functioning here and abroad. (Later in the book an explanation of how the Institute is structured and operates will be given.) In the few schools that have adopted the concept, healing has begun to take place. Optimism is beginning to replace skepticism in the teachers' lounge.

Unfortunately, however, school officials continue to scramble for a solution to a problem that seems overwhelming – beyond their ability to solve. As a consequence, they are willing to settle for anything that will tranquilize the school's social condition. To them, that's more important than analyzing the problem and finding ways to solve it, and it is understandable why they feel that way. Their immediate responsibility is to provide a healthy environment so that students can achieve academically. Racial tensions in school upset the learning environment.

Many school boards believe that by stressing multiculturalism in the classroom, minorities in school and in the community at large will be less likely to create trouble. Multiculturalism has become the "in" word; it is being hailed as the race relations panacea. As a result a new service industry has been spawned. Many human resource management firms have added race relations to their list of offerings. And new companies have sprung up, producing multicultural education workshops and print and audio-visual materials. They bombard schools with fliers and brochures, asking and getting high fees.

Sadly, very little substantial change results from these efforts. The infection and wounds remain; and the enthusiasm among teachers to attend another workshop lessens. Though few will say it openly, most of the workshop participants secretly believe there is little anyone can do to change people's racial attitudes. As a result, many teachers go about promoting multiculturalism without much conviction. In fact, there are those who resent having to do it. Those feelings of reservation and resentment don't go unnoticed by the students.

While multiculturalism, as it is practiced in most schools today, can be a step in the right direction, it can also become a detriment to achieving racial unity. This point was reinforced for me at a meeting I attended in Canada. The executive director of a race relations council in Greater Toronto, a black man originally from South Africa, stood up and said, "Multiculturalism, as it is taught in our schools, will lead to sophisticated apartheid."

That was already happening in Britain in 1989, when I arrived to do a series of lectures, and promote my book, *To Be One*. Rocked by a rash of racial unrest in its schools, the national government launched a heavily-financed multicultural education program to be carried out by every school in the country. Funds for curriculum and materials development were funneled to the major minorities. While black and Asian students were gaining a better appreciation of their own particular cultures, two frightening results were becoming apparent. A warped pride developed of each group's culture, creating invisible and impenetrable barriers between them; and there was backlash among white students. The whites resented not receiving the attention that the students of color were getting. During my lecture tour, I learned of a racial incident in a Manchester school that led to a student's death.

123

I knew why the multicultural education scheme was failing, and shared my views during an address in Liverpool. The director of the city's race relations board was in the audience. (The board advises the local government and school system on racial matters.)

In my talk I pointed out that while it is important for everyone to have a healthy understanding of one's cultural heritage, and an appreciation of other cultures, it is more important to have an understanding of the principle of the oneness of humanity. To ignore oneness and stress diversity can only lead to a "sophisticated apartheid," which is manifested by children thinking that their culture is better than everyone else's. Cultural superiority, whether expressed openly or felt in silence, creates psychological barriers in a community. Students must know that all members of the human race, regardless of skin color, surname and language, belong to the human family.

By internalizing the principle of the oneness of humankind you develop a built-in safeguard against a culturally superior attitude. You acquire an eye for beauty and goodness wherever it appears – and compassion for those cultures that are prevented from expressing themselves freely by the forces of oppression. Without a belief in the oneness of humankind it is impossible to develop a genuine appreciation for diversity. Trying to do so would be like expecting a rootless plant to grow. Only when students gain that understanding will they disengage themselves from the clutches of cultural chauvinism and truly appreciate and celebrate cultural diversity. They must understand that the principle of unity and diversity is a law of life. When understood and practiced, it becomes a vaccine against the disease of racism.

After the Liverpool talk, the race relations board director, a man of Pakistani background, came up to me, clasped my hand with both of his, and said, "Thank you! Thank you! I see what we have been missing – we must emphasize oneness and unity as well as an appreciation for diversity in our schools."

When I returned home, I discovered there were organizations that fostered multiculturalism as a means of preventing unity. To them, the idea of assimilation is an anathema; they fear it would lead to the dissolution of their culture – and advantage – in society. Their aim is to create a sense of tolerance between groups, to allow each group to do what it wishes to do without any interference from anyone else. Some of these organizations have produced slick, well financed programs that desperate school systems buy, thinking it will solve their "racial problem."

Frankly, I'm opposed to this approach on humanitarian grounds. I can't in good conscience tolerate cultural customs that violate human rights and perpetuate social injustice. Some cultures, for example, support a strict caste system. In India, according to custom, an Untouchable isn't allowed to step in the shadow of a Brahmin. To do so could lead to the Untouchable's death, with the authorities looking the other way. Nor can I tolerate a cultural custom that calls for young women who reach puberty to undergo a physically painful and psychologically damaging circumcision rite, unjustified by any medical reasoning. What is equally distasteful is the "chosen people" status that some cultures claim. All humans are God's children.

While I could appreciate the fear that prompted these organizations to take the toleration approach, I found it to be another Band-Aid solution to a social illness that requires a potent medicine. Toleration, I felt, would only lead to a truce that could easily be upset by a rumor or an irrational act. What is necessary is for people everywhere to recognize, once and for all, the truth – that we are all members of the same family, that our family must be united if we are to have peace in the world, and that learning to love one another, which is an essential step toward unity, is our greatest challenge.

Because I felt that education would be the most effective vehicle to get this message across, I vowed to put together a position paper that would explain why it was important to integrate the principles of the oneness of humankind and unity and diversity into school curricula. It dawned on me that educators should know that the principle of the oneness of humankind should be taught in schools, not only because it would be an antidote against racism, but also because it is the truth. Isn't one of the missions of a school to expose its students to the truth? If science accepts this truth, shouldn't educators feel obligated to share this knowledge with their students? By depriving children of this truth, teachers are guilty of perpetuating ignorance in the guise of knowledge.

I envisioned kindergartners, even pre-school children, – blacks, Asians, whites, Latinos and American Indians – learning that they were all related, members of the same family. And that this truth would be reinforced throughout their elementary and high school years, reflected in every subject they took, even physical education.

Why the saturation approach? Because in America the citizenry has been brainwashed for centuries into believing that whites are inherently superior to people of color. After twelve years of an education that features the unity and diversity principle, students would graduate with a different social outlook than the graduates of the past. They would understand and practice the oneness of humanity principle. Unlike the previous generation of youth, they would be free of the infection and wounds of racism. I grew excited at the prospect of every school in America, better yet, every school in the world, adopting this idea.

That was my dream. The first step to implementing it was to prepare the position paper. I knew I shouldn't do it alone, for I had little experience in drafting curricula; and what was needed was someone with a strong scientific background who had quick access to data that proves that every human being belongs to the same family. Also, I have learned through my experience as a Bahá'í, that mature group consultation can shed more light than the effort of a single mind.

I knew that it wouldn't be easy to assemble the group, because all of its members had to believe in the concept, and be willing to find time to work on the project. And the fact that it wasn't a money-making proposition would be an obstacle.

Of the first group I assembled, four of the five members soon left for one reason or another. The fifth remained, and was joined by four replacements who continued with the project. In addition to myself, the members of this group were Brian Aull, an electrical engineer who works at Lincoln Laboratory in Lexington, Massachusetts; Barbara Hacker, a teacher for a Montessori School in Houston; Robert Postlethwaite, a Harvard graduate student at the time, and now a professor at a Chinese university; and my son, Tod Rutstein, an educator at the Baltimore Friends School in Baltimore.

Through consultation we arrived at a structure for the paper. The first section would explain the need for what we were proposing. That would be followed with scientific proofs of the oneness of humankind and an explanation of the principle of unity in diversity in nature. The next section would be devoted to describing how the principles of the oneness of humankind and unity in diversity can be integrated into mathematics, literature, science, history and other subjects.

While we provided this information, we pointed out that, for the best results, the teachers themselves should consult and arrive at original approaches with which they would feel comfortable. Why? Because teachers have a tendency to be more enthusiastic about carrying out their own ideas than ideas of someone who isn't familiar with their classroom conditions. The last section would provide information on how to get teachers and administrators committed to the project.

We wanted to produce a document that would set off a positive reaction from public school system superintendents and independent school principals. We wanted them to see why the step beyond multiculturalism was essential to achieving racial harmony. As far as we knew no educationalist had advocated taking such a step.

Before preparing the final draft, we solicited advice from black, Hispanic, and white teachers and administrators who believed in the concept. Their guidance on what psychological approach to take was extremely helpful. We gave ourselves two months to complete the paper. After several all-day meetings, we divided the tasks among the five of us. What we researched and wrote was based on our interests and strengths in the education and human relations fields.

127

While none of us were recognized experts in those fields, we believed in the concept, and saw how it could contribute significantly to eventually overcoming racism in a community, and be an important factor in unifying it. That vision – and faith – drove us to complete the paper, "Healing Racism: Education's Role."

The document was kept short, because those whom we wanted to reach were busy people. Anything over twenty pages, especially from unknowns in the field, would end up collecting dust on a shelf.

In three years, thousands of copies have been circulated throughout the Americas; some have surfaced in Europe and the Pacific Islands. So far, a few schools are implementing what the position paper calls for.

U niversities and colleges can play an important role in healing the disease of racism. I'm not talking about instituting a mandatory course on diversity appreciation. While that's nice, it's not going to rid us of our infection or wounds. Courses should be offered that expose students to the oneness of humankind principle.

College departments of education should be training prospective and practicing teachers on how to weave the principals of the oneness of humanity and unity in diversity into every subject taught from kindergarten to twelfth grade. To make it easier for the professionals, classes should be given in the schools where they teach.

A course on how teachers can set up, structure and participate in an Institute for the Healing of Racism should also be offered. Since racism won't be eradicated overnight, a special master's degree program should be established that would produce a school race-relations specialist. I'm not talking about an affirmative action expert whose primary duty is to hire minority educators and settle racial disputes. External solutions won't solve internal problems. To qualify for the program, the candidate must know the nature and causes of the problem, have healing qualities, be compassionate and not judgmental, have an understanding of the pain racism generates in people of color and whites, and be a peace-maker and a force for unity.

This person would be trained to inspire the faculty to participate in an Institute – and assist in its development. And the specialist would oversee the teaching of the oneness of humankind effort and organize outreach programs like special race-relations workshops for parents. Through this individual, schools would become centers of racial healing in the community.

I believe that if every school taught the oneness of humankind and the unity in diversity principles, and operated an Institute for the Healing of Racism for its teachers, racism would be eliminated in America in one or two generations.

13
Birth of the Institute

Some might say that the creation of the Institute for the Healing of Racism concept was a classic case of serendipity. For its conception was not the result of a high-powered strategy meeting held by leading race relations thinkers and officials. It was not the brainchild of an established social activist agency – or a famous civil rights leader. And it certainly wasn't plotted by the Bahá'í leadership as a means of gaining converts to its faith – as some critics claim.

It came about because some Bahá'ís, mostly black and white women, around the same time, in different parts of the country, were terribly frustrated with the lack of progress in overcoming racism – and wanted to do something constructive about it. We later discovered that our observations of the nation's racial condition were in sync: Because of racism the soul of America was eroding, and the remedies being tried were ineffective. In fact, the gulf between the black and white communities was widening; and the animosity between them intensifying. What made matters worse was that the nation's leadership had no real solutions. But something had to be done – soon, we felt. Blacks were growing less patient, and demanding that they be freed from the shackles of hopelessness; some well meaning whites, on the other hand, were groping blindly for ways to unite both communities, and meeting what seemed to be insurmountable obstacles at every turn.

Though we had no influence with important decision-makers, we had a strong sense of what the problem was, and what was needed to solve it. As Bahá'ís, we believed that everyone on the planet was a member of the family of man; that an understanding of this principle on the part of the citizenry would go a long way in eradicating racism. We were also aware of the fact that the lack of headway in breaking down racial barriers was due to ignorance of the nature of the problem, especially among whites. We knew that racism was a disease, and that healing was required. Trying to treat others when we were either infected or wounded ourselves was, at first, a stumbling block. It seemed so hypocritical. But we soon overcame that hurdle when we realized that doing nothing wasn't going to help us or anyone else. With lots of faith and pure motives, we began to consult and experiment on how to go about healing the disease of racism. Workable formats began to evolve, despite the fact that none of us were race relations experts.

T he reaction to my book, *To Be One*, was the catalyst that drove me to do what I had wanted to do for years but lacked the courage and guidance to do. Black and white men and women were asking me for help. When a close psychiatrist friend revealed what impact my book had on him and asked me what can be done to help people like himself, I began to search for solutions. I knew we were dealing with a disease, but not a physical one; it was more of a psychological disorder, like alcoholism. The term Racism Anonymous came to mind. When I shared the name with some of my journalist friends, they approved of it, thinking it was "catchy."

But I had a serious problem. While I thought I had a good name for an anti-racism campaign, I felt like the novice baker who knew how to make custard, but lacked the knowledge to make the rest of the chocolate eclair. Not being a psychologist or psychiatrist, I couldn't articulate effectively the disease's pathology. But that didn't discourage me from trying to create a healing method. Deep down I knew it was the right thing to do. I immediately contacted a number of friends and associates who were professionals in the behavioral sciences. Their response to my appeal for help was disappointing. They didn't share my enthusiasm for the idea; in fact, they were terribly condescending, and pessimistic as to its chances of succeeding. Some gave me the impression of being skeptical spectators waiting for me to fail.

I prayed for help. And the guidance seemed to come in stages; as always, not in the form I had anticipated. Apparently I needed some psychological shoring-up before embarking on an anti-racism campaign that was yet to be defined. The shoring-up occurred in Liverpool, England, in early 1989. I was in the midst of a lecture series, when I met a remarkable Malaysian gentleman who volunteered some advice on the kind of attitude that's required before starting a social development project. "Do not think about the reasons why it cannot be done," he said, "think about the reasons why it can be done – and, for God's sake, do it!"

During the remainder of the tour I worked at internalizing the advice, which made a lot of sense to me. But it wasn't easy to do. It was difficult trying to ignore my shortcomings and the obvious pitfalls I would encounter in starting a campaign. I really believe that because I viewed the Malaysian man's advice as an answer to my prayer, I was able to overcome most of my reservations and press onward, assured that what I thought needed to be done would eventually materialize.

Shortly after my return home, I received a phone call from a woman in Houston, whom I didn't know. Hitaji Aziz, who was a radio talk-show host, said a mutual friend of ours suggested that she contact me with an anti-racism idea. "I have been reading portions of *To Be One* over the air," she said, "and the response from blacks and whites has been overwhelming. They're seeking help.

"Since I'm a recovering alcoholic and have some counseling experience, I thought we could set up Racism Anonymous chapters around the country. What do you think?"

Elated, I said, "Frankly, you are an answer to my prayers. I had come up with the same idea several weeks ago, and was looking for someone to collaborate with."

"Great!" she said. "A number of us down here are trying to organize an ongoing workshop. Your book has been very helpful. Perhaps we can work together."

I was encouraged. A few weeks later I would be giving a workshop on racism at the University of Texas at Austin. The fact that

Hitaji Aziz and her compatriots didn't show up didn't bother me, because they were back in Houston, sponsoring a racism workshop of their own.

It was a whirlwind weekend. Besides the workshop, I had to appear on a public panel at the university with the state's assistant attorney general, a history professor and the head of the NAACP's regional office. And there were television and radio interviews and a session with a newspaper reporter.

I don't know what possessed me – but, near the end of my stay in Austin, I challenged the workshop participants to start Racism Anonymous groups where they lived. I did that without knowing how the groups should be structured. All I knew was that men and women who recognized that they were infected or wounded by racism needed a forum where they could help each other heal.

Because I knew of Alcoholics Anonymous' success rate, I suggested that perhaps the participants employ some of that organization's techniques. And that advice was given with very little understanding of AA's structure. Call it simple faith, but I felt that if the participants were sincere in their desire to heal, if they were patient and persistent, kind toward each other and willing to listen to each other without being offended, they would gain direction as to how to structure their groups. They would evolve organically. In fact, I believed that expending a lot of energy on structuring would take valuable time from the healing process. Besides, a tightly structured procedure usually stifles spontaneity, and inhibits full and free expression and dialogue.

As a result of the workshop, two programs for healing were established, one in San Marcos, and the other on the campus of the university, sponsored by the Bahá'í Association and the Texas Union Multicultural Task Force. Two seeds had been planted, and I didn't have the foggiest notion as to how they would grow.

When I returned home, I discovered that another seed had been planted in Texas. I received a phone call from Jackie Cone in

Houston, who declared that their group was calling itself the Institute for the Healing of Racism. "A much better name than Racism Anonymous," I told her, and the new name is now in general use.

During the past three years I have developed a close relationship with the Houston group. I went there three times, each time as their guest speaker. Each trip was a moving learning experience for me. For I witnessed how honesty, conviction, courage and a deep desire to do good can compensate for a lack of expertise in healing our infection and wounds. Because of their sincerity and absolute devotion to their cause, I believe, they drew assistance from a force beyond this earthly plane. They triumphed despite seemingly insurmountable obstacles. Though from different cultural, economic and educational backgrounds, the Institute members were united in thought and had their sights focused on a vision they created through consultation.

While they had a healthy understanding of the problem they were committed to solving, they never felt they had all of the answers. They had an idea of how the answers could be developed. It would take a process, they felt. Creating the process wasn't easy, for there was opposition from close friends and institutions they respected. What hurt most was that some of the opposition was coming from people who they thought would be the first to applaud what they had set out to do.

Their critics felt the Institute members weren't qualified to carry out their mission; that they were mischief-makers; that they would end up doing more harm than good, creating disunity in the community; that they were setting themselves up as race relations experts in a field in which they had little experience, thus giving the impression of being superior to those who didn't share their views.

Because the opposition was unexpected, confronting it consumed a lot of energy, and caused considerable grief. But, in time, bridges of understanding were built, and most of those who had been critical became supportive of the Institute, and some even became involved in its program.

Houston's Institute for the Healing of Racism has worked hard in developing clear focus and purpose. It has created a curriculum for its nine-week series of workshops, called Dialogue. Meeting weekly, the members discuss topics like the difference between prejudice and racism; how racism is perpetuated through early childhood experiences; misinformation and segregation; unaware racism – we have all been affected; internalized racism – when the anger, hurt and frustration turn inward; stereotypes and how they affect us; institutionalized racism, consisting of the systems that affect us daily – media, legal, school, health care, economics; the oneness of humanity; achieving unity and preserving diversity; and ally-building as a way to heal – an individual commitment.

The Dialogue series is repeated after a two-week hiatus. Interestingly, during the layoff period, the workshop participants – black, white, Asian, American Indian, and Latino – demonstrate a need to be together. They do things socially, hold dinner parties, go to the movies. They find themselves doing things they would never have done prior to their Dialogue experience. What they discover is that they have become a genuine force for unity.

Often, those who take the series of workshops take them two or three times. Dialogue is given throughout the year.

Because of its success, Houston's Institute for the Healing of Racism has been asked by like-minded men and women in different cities to help them set up a similar program. Teams have been organized to help establish Institutes in different places. Every team is composed of people of color and whites.

While the Houston group has met with considerable success, many of the other Institutes throughout North America have developed their own methods and techniques. In fact, some have studied Houston's format and Dialogue curriculum and decided not to use them, creating instead approaches better suited to their communities.

Despite their growing number, Institutes for the Healing of

135

Racism aren't part of a monolithic organization that demands uniformity of operations. While they are autonomous, they do make a concerted effort to exchange information with each other. In September of 1991, Houston's Institute organized a national conference. Ninety-six representatives from many states showed up – some coming from as far away as California, Oregon, Illinois, Massachusetts, South Carolina, Maryland and New York.

It was a time for sharing success stories, which bolstered our resolve to forge ahead. Participants sought and received help in solving problems that their Institutes were facing. Healthy networking was accomplished. Everyone agreed that a central clearinghouse was needed that would produce a monthly newsletter, organize future conferences, and exchange the kind of information that Institutes everywhere would find useful. Some envisioned the clearinghouse evolving into a research and development center on race relations, which would include a library with an audio- and video cassette-producing facility.

14
Fire of Hope

Not all of the Institutes for the Healing of Racism which have been established have reached maturity. In fact, some are still struggling, making slow headway. But one thing is clear: All of the participants are gaining something positive from the experience, even those who can't discern the benefits. Their passion for swift progress blinds them from seeing the progress that has already been made.

This became apparent when I met with the steering committee of one of the Institutes in the South. They were bemoaning the fact that only twenty to twenty-five people were attending their sharing sessions.

"How long have you been functioning?" I asked.

"Almost five months," said one of the members.

"Are most of the attendees regulars?"

"About fifteen, with five or six new ones each session."

"That's marvelous."

A young white man was shaking his head, obviously in disagreement with me. "At that rate," he said, "we won't make a dent. There are nearly four hundred thousand people in this city."

"I know you're anxious. In a way, that's healthy, because that will keep you persistent. But patience is required also. In fact, its just as important as persistence," I said. "Remember, racism has been around for a long time."

"I know," the young man shot back, "but there are a lot of folks hurting out there, and, frankly, they're tired of being patient."

"I'm aware," I said. "But if we give up, then no one will be healed, and you'll join the bandwagon of complainers who curse the darkness instead of lighting candles.

"We must keep our campaign in perspective. Racism won't be eliminated quickly. Dogged determination is required. If we keep our objectives in sight and maintain patience and persistence, significant progress will be made. At this point in your development, numbers aren't as important as to what is happening to those who participate regularly."

"Why?" asked a black woman.

"Because there isn't another organization in this city that's trying to heal the infection and wounds of racism of its membership, and that can break down social barriers. Your Institute is a unique social dynamic.

"Look at who is gathered in this room. An African-American Christian man who is a lay leader in the largest black church in the city; a white Methodist male computer programmer; a black grandmother who is a recent convert to Sunni Islam; a couple of black and white Bahá'ís; and a black college professor."

The black grandmother chuckled, "It is a miracle."

"Absolutely!" I said.

The African-American Christian shook his head in wonderment: "Never before have I been so at ease with white folks as I am with you all. I can be myself. I know that people are really listening and appreciating what I have to say. It is like being with family – no, better than that!"

After the others confirmed what the black Christian gentleman said, I pointed out that people are watching what the Institute is doing. "While the cynics are waiting for it to fizzle, there are folks who are looking to be healed but are afraid of becoming a part of something that might disappoint them. They probably were disappointed in the past. When they hear of your success they will join you, and then the more timid will follow," I said.

"What is most important is keeping the fire of hope that you have started going."

One of the Bahá'ís said, "I guess we have received great news media coverage, because they view what we're doing as unprecedented for this city. They see the fire."

"My God," I said, "though you are a small group, without any political clout, the leading daily newspaper has done several articles on you, including a feature in its Sunday magazine section. You've been interviewed on television. There have been stories on the TV and radio news. And all of it favorable!"

The black college professor smiled and said, "The more favorable publicity we receive, the more legitimate we appear to the public, and that should draw more people of good will to the Institute."

"Right!" said the white computer programmer.

Sharing what some of the more established Institutes were accomplishing also helped to lift the spirits of the members of the steering committee. They were impressed that the Vietnamese community in a large city in the Southwest turned to the Institute for help when a Vietnamese child was murdered by some Skinheads; that the Institute in Binghamton, New York, has received a grant from IBM, is networking with the Elmira YWCA and is working with the Black Student Association at the University of New York at Binghampton in setting up a free computer training program for unemployed young adults; that teachers have established Institutes for the Healing of Racism in their schools; and that mayors, district attorneys, and police chiefs have asked Institutes for help.

What really impressed the steering committee was the January 1992 report published by the Houston Institute, revealing some of the interest it has generated in its region.

"We are continually called on to make presentations or offer workshops dealing with racial issues," the report says. "Requests have come from Houston Police Academy, Dupont, Inc., Conoco Petroleum Company's Legal Department, the city Health Department, Office of the Mayor, several community colleges, several university schools of social work, peace groups, Unitarian, Baptist, Methodist groups, the Galveston-Houston Roman Catholic Diocese, Rotary Club, elementary schools, and high school student groups working to combat racism.

"University professors assign their students to attend sessions, and one high school teacher 50 miles from Houston rented a bus to bring his students to Dialogue. The University of Houston Bahá'í Club sponsored a successful Dialogue series on campus with Institute facilitators. We are talking with Houston Community College about a possibility of providing Dialogue to 1,000 people. In October, Institute representatives will present a workshop at the Carter G. Woodson Foundation Conference in Kansas City. The event will draw 700 African-Americans. We have not solicited any of these contacts. They have come to us."

The report notes that the bishop of the Houston-Galveston Roman Catholic Diocese had called the Institute to request consultation and assistance.

"He feels that the diversity workshops and sensitivity training sessions that they hold are not effecting the change which they want to see. He feels that the approach we use is more effective in that it gets to the heart of the problem," the report says.

15
Ground Rules

While not every Institute employs the same format, the goal is the same – racial unity in the community. The major objective to achieving the goal is the healing of the disease and wounds of racism. If the major objective is ignored, then the goal is impossible to achieve.

All Institutes try to acquaint the participants with the nature of the problem, and how to solve it – the primary thrust being the healing of oneself. Without being engaged in self-healing, you can't effectively help others to heal. There are four steps in the process:

1. To explain how racism came into being in America.

This is essential to the healing process. With an understanding of true American history – not the propaganda children are spoon-fed in most schools – racism's victims (people of color *and* whites) realize that being infected or wounded by racism isn't their fault. As a consequence, they begin to shed the mask of denial, and begin to appreciate the notion that racism is a sickness, and they entertain the idea of seeking help. At that point they are ready to take the next step in the healing process.

2. To gain an understanding of the pathology of the disease of racism, and what constitutes the wounds.

This is necessary to healing, for it removes from the white man the stigma of being evil. Instead, he views himself as sick. There is no longer the need to deny his inherent and subconscious feeling of superiority toward blacks. He is emotionally better prepared to seek a cure.

Not seeking a cure, he realizes, would be like a person stricken with pneumonia refusing medical help. As for the black person, he learns what his wounds are and what he must do to overcome them. This is important, because without that knowledge he won't know what needs healing. His denial will stand in the way.

3. To provide a place where the infected and wounded come together to help heal each other.

In this setting, no one group is dominant. Everyone is equal – for all are sick, seeking a cure. As a consequence, participants of color find the situation comfortable, allowing them to share with white folks what they normally wouldn't share with them. They're not subject to the patronizing attitude or the superior air of the white person who is plagued by denial.

The healing process is actually a series of heartfelt sharing sessions, where listening is as important as telling. Listening with the heart, as well as the ear, is stressed. What is shared isn't judged by anyone. Yet, considerable learning goes on. When the festering infection and wounds rise from the unconscious to the conscious level, understanding is generated, a kind of understanding that sparks a sense of liberation. Emotional barriers between people collapse.

What usually happens is that, when a white person is exposed to the black person's pain, a natural urge to reach out to the black person wells up in the white person. The same thing happens to a black person when he's exposed to the white person's sincere struggle to free himself of his infection. Two souls who were worlds apart have been brought together. For the first time, they can naturally respond to each other with appropriate compassion and support founded on unconditional love. They experience real unity – a unity that springs from an interior impulse, not external stimulation.

Yes, the Institute for the Healing of Racism provides the forum for the development of racial unity. I know of no other place where the mechanics of unity are truly exercised – unlike the race unity rallies and picnics I have attended, where men and women of different skin color mingle, trying hard to conceal their infection and wounds, while forcing themselves to smile and be politically correct for an hour or two.

No one is coerced to say anything during the sharing sessions. It is purely voluntary expression, usually stimulated by the facilitator's synopsis of a topic or a statement made by a fellow participant. In a trusting atmosphere, the participants who have overcome their denial don't hesitate to share their true feelings. They feel comfortable because their honest expressions are not viewed as a form of confession, but, rather, symptoms of a disease or wound that most human beings have been afflicted with unwittingly. In understanding this point, it might be helpful to consider the process of any other disease. Would it be appropriate to view a cancer patient as blameworthy for his or her symptoms? Would it be sensible to encourage denial of the reality of the ailment, all the while operating under the notion that the affliction is a sin? Absolutely not.

Of course, members of an Institute don't use this analogy to lose sight of the moral nature of the problem. It simply helps to destroy guilt, which is an unproductive emotion. It doesn't absolve anyone from responsibility.

In the light of this perspective, it is easy to recognize that the Institute provides women and men with an opportunity to make a sincere attempt to cure their sickness. Their sharing is not only a way to relieve inner pain, it is also an appeal for help. Others in the group respond sympathetically.

4. To forge genuine friendships through discoursing, as the group evolves into a dependable force for social action.

Each member has become a social activist without trying to be one. The sharing process generates in the participants a will and enthusiasm for sharing the healing experience with the community at large. They want everyone to enjoy the freedom they know all people have the potential of experiencing. Sustained by that kind of spirit, they don't suffer from burnout.

They may get tired and have to relax for a while, but their relaxation period is used to regenerate the energy needed to promote the cause. Armed with the knowledge of how hurtful racism is to a person and a community, members of Institutes, as we mentioned earlier, become highly motivated to work to foster racial unity in towns where they live.

Some Institutes involve themselves by promoting their principles through working with local school systems. They have been successful in getting a number of public, parochial and independent schools to adopt the position paper, "Healing Racism: Education's Role," as a means of combating racism in the classroom. Institutes also become involved in working with police and health departments, with district attorneys' offices, corporations and colleges, and setting up special workshops that help black males gain greater self-esteem.

Some community leaders have identified the Institute for the Healing of Racism as an idea whose time has come. In Nashville, Tennessee, Acting Assistant Police Chief William D. Hamblin, remarked on the Institute's effectiveness: "I see it becoming just as essential to police employee training as any stress management curriculum or personal self-defense training."

Support of the healing concept has also come from the grandson of Mohandas K. Gandhi, whose philosophy of nonviolence as an instrument to overcome oppression has changed the world, and has been at the heart of the American Civil Rights Movement. Arun Gandhi has been a participant in a healing Institute in Memphis – where he founded the M.K. Gandhi Institute for the Study of Non-Violence. He said of the Memphis Institute for the Healing of Racism, "The approach is one that I find very interesting and encouraging. I have always felt that a dialogue between people is the best way to resolve many of the conflicts that exist, and the Institute is a good forum for dialogue. I think it has a great potential for bringing people together and opening hearts."

Those of us who have been involved with the Institute for the Healing of Racism from its inception know from experience that any attempt to broaden our target to include all of the other prejudices – like sexism – seriously weakens the organization's effectiveness. What usually happens is that many of the participants of color, especially blacks, don't come to the sessions anymore. Trying to deal with all forms of oppression at once, they feel, is an attempt by whites to distance themselves from the core of the racism problem. For me, a middle-aged black woman's comments concerning this issue made a lot of sense. "All of these isms are bad, and they should be done away with – but they're all different," she said. "A smart doctor doesn't treat a breast cancer patient and someone suffering from heart disease with the same medicine."

As for political action? The Institute for the Healing of Racism has nothing to do with politics. Its primary focus is on healing. There are plenty of political action groups, but not many organizations involved in curing the infection and wounds of racism. Anyone who tries to create a political power base is asked to desist. If the request is ignored, the person is dropped from membership. In fact, the Institutes forbid anyone from trying to promote an ideology, cause, or religion during the sharing sessions, or any other meeting held by the Institute. A way to discourage this from happening is for the facilitator to go over the Institute's purposes and ground rules before each session. That kind of repetitive focus is essential, for most of us are creatures of habit that need reminders to avoid resorting to behavioral patterns that could disrupt a sharing session.

In the past three years, Institutes have created behavioral and attitudinal guidelines for sharing and listening. Guidelines have also been drafted for facilitators. Both sets of guidelines are distributed when the Institute is formed, and given to every newcomer.

Though the Institute for the Healing of Racism concept was created by a group of Bahá'ís, it was not our intent to use it as a proselytizing vehicle. It was designed to be a social development

145

service to the community at large. Our hope was that women and men of all faiths, as well as those who have no religious affiliation, would join in a community effort to eliminate the epidemic of racism in their town. So far, that has happened.

Forming a new Institute is simple, once you have the commitment of at least a few individuals. But the right conditions are necessary for getting started. It is important for those involved to embrace the basic premises of the Institute model (see appendix). Of course, there is no required method for organizing, but what has worked well so far is to take advantage of the enthusiasm generated from an opening meeting, where the gravity of the problem is presented and discussed.

Names, addresses and telephone numbers of all those who want to join are recorded. A follow-up session is scheduled soon afterwards so the members can quickly create their objectives, structure and format. A permanent steering committee usually results from this session. Composed of five to seven deeply committed members, the committee oversees logistical matters, like finding a meeting place, notifying the membership of special meetings, producing a newsletter, taking care of correspondence, setting policy and safeguarding the Institute's integrity. Those who serve on the steering committee don't view their membership as a position of power, but rather, an opportunity to be of greater service. No big fuss is made over who serves on the steering committee. It's usually the people who have the time and commitment to do it.

It is important to note that many of those who signed up to be a part of the Institute may not appear at the first meeting. This is not because they have lost interest. They are being cautious, carefully watching to see if the Institute has legitimate staying power. If it continues to function, and is making headway in achieving its goals, it will attract new participants, including some with reservations. Leading community officials will take notice, and either join or openly support the group's efforts; and public and private agencies will solicit the aid of the Institute to help them create a healthier social climate within their precincts.

16
Signs of Willingness

In North America it's difficult to avoid racism. If it isn't blatantly obvious – like graffiti in gymnasium locker rooms – it festers beneath the surface of a community that has never experienced "racial trouble," manifesting itself from time to time, and reminding those of us who want to wish racism away that it can't be done.

Lionel, a white teenager, living in an essentially middle-class community, was shocked to learn that his town was infected. Outwardly, his hometown seemed progressive. It had an active United Nations Association chapter. Human Rights Day was celebrated every year, always producing a big turnout. More than ninety percent of the townspeople gave annually to the United Way.

The shock occurred when he and his two closest friends – both black – were downtown, trying to hail a cab on a cold, windy day. In about an hour, more than ten empty cabs passed by. Some had slowed down, and then roared by when the drivers got a close look at the three young men. Though Lionel and his friends, Leonard and Willie, never discussed why they were unable to hail a cab, they understood why. It took a call to Willie's father to get them home. What angered Lionel was that he didn't know how to prevent cab drivers from doing that sort of thing again.

Even families that try to avoid the effects of racism are reminded that there's no place to escape from it. A Washington state family thought they had found the place when they moved out of Seattle's inner city to a pleasant white suburb. It didn't take long before they realized that the specter of racism had cast its shadow over the town they had moved to. The two teenage children had encounters with the police. Not that they had done anything wrong. Rosemary was stopped by the police as she was walking home from the mall. She was wearing normal-looking jogging clothes and carried an envelope of film from the camera store. It was early evening, still light.

Two white policemen stopped their car, got out, and followed her on foot along the street. The first question out of their mouths was, "What are you doing in this neighborhood?"

The officers proceeded to interrogate Rosemary with questions like, "Where do you live? What do your parents do for a living? Do they own or rent the house you live in?"

They demanded that they be allowed to look inside the envelope she was carrying, and inspect its contents. Rosemary asked them if she had done anything wrong. "No, you can go," they said.

Three weeks later Rosemary's brother, Eric, had a similar experience. Outraged, their father called on the police chief to complain.

The chief denied that his department discriminated against African-Americans, and stated that it was the duty of the police to stop and question anyone who looked "curious" or "suspicious." He went on to say that it was the goal of his department to be very aggressive in making stops and in collecting "field investigation" data.

"So," asked her agitated father, "if Rosemary were a blonde, white woman your police officers would have stopped her all the same?"

The police chief refused to answer the question. He merely said, "Our policy is to stop anyone who is curious and suspicious."

Under stressful circumstances, racist acts will erupt in the most unlikely places, especially when one's primacy is threatened. Longmeadow, Massachusetts, is a fashionable suburb of Springfield, the largest city in the western part of the state. Longmeadow's population is highly educated and well-to-do, with a strong interest in the arts and philanthropy. I'm sure that the great majority of people there are openly opposed to the Ku Klux Klan and would be among the first to sign petitions calling for the prosecution of a lynch mob living in a different state.

When Springfield's Central High School basketball team – a perennial powerhouse in the state – came to play Longmeadow's team in 1991, lots of townspeople turned out to see their boys pull the upset of the year. Well, Longmeadow didn't even come close to pulling an upset.

The boys from Springfield – mostly blacks and Latinos – were beating their white hosts by more than forty points near the end of game. Frustrated, the fans suddenly broke out in a chant directed at the Central High School team. "It's all right, its okay, you will work for us someday."

What was festering in the unconscious rose to the conscious level. Emotionally upset, the fans could no longer restrain themselves. Their true feelings had to be expressed when their dominance over people they believed inferior to them was being threatened.

Even newspapers that editorially oppose racism are unable to conceal their infection all of the time. It occasionally oozes onto the editorial pages, unrecognized by most white reporters and editors.

In an editorial on October 30, 1991, for example, the Springfield Union-News, the city's only daily, endorsed eight candidates for the nine-member City Council. It explained that the election to the ninth seat of any one of four black challengers also running would serve the purpose of adding to "the ethnic diversity of the council," on which only one black was already serving.

While the newspaper obviously didn't sense the insult contained in the grab-bag method it recommended for filling the ninth seat, the candidates and the rest of the black community felt it keenly. One of the challengers complained, in a letter to the editor, that "the statement 'you pick one of the four' does not reflect the fact that they are some of the best qualified candidates who have come forward..." Another letter-writer said that the editorial was "patronizing and insidiously racist," and that "urging voters to simply pick one of these four candidates as though they were items on a Chinese restaurant's menu is a copout."

The newspaper responded to the criticism by saying all four candidates were well qualified, and "we could not choose one, or even two of them, above the others."

"Far from being racist, our decision is one of affirmative action," the newspaper said, apologizing only for what it said was its failure to communicate its message effectively.

Here is a case of a distinguished newspaper that prides itself on being a long-time advocate of human rights exposing its true feelings about the black community within the city it serves. The two editorials involved are classic examples of the deep-seated institutionalized race prejudice that exists in America. I'm sure that many other newspapers are making similar insensitive social blunders. And what's scary is that they're not aware of what they're doing. They are prisoners of denial. Unaware that their inherent and subconscious feeling of superiority toward blacks is reflected in their editorial attempts to heal a social ill, their comments usually keep alive the racist feelings within the white community.

How? Take, for example, the editorials in question. Their underlying message, I feel, is that black candidates for political office don't deserve the same kind of scrutiny as their white counterparts because they are of less value. Having another black on the City Council would fulfill a social cosmetic requirement, and give the impression that the city's governing body is democratic.

These slights toward blacks that I have shared with you are not exceptions to the rule. Similar acts occur across the land on a daily basis by people who aren't congenital haters. They're not bigots, nor do they subscribe to white supremacy theories. They are, by and large, decent human beings who have expressed compassion, kindness and love in their lives, not only to their family members, but to strangers as well. Yet, in their dealings with blacks, the symptoms of their infection break out, often unbeknownst to them. Of course, continual exposure to these symptoms takes its toll on blacks. While it isn't something they can shrug off, attempts are made to do just that in a variety of ways. It isn't easy to try to make the best of it when empty taxi cabs refuse to pick you up because of your skin color.

Imagine how the Central High School basketball team felt when the Longmeadow fans expressed their feelings of superiority toward them in the form of that chant. I'm sure most of the fans would never classify their behavior that night as a racist act.

As I see it, it isn't the activity of the Ku Klux Klan that is the major problem. The KKK is only an extreme extension of the real problem, a problem most Americans refuse to recognize. And that is: We live in a fundamentally racist nation, founded by racist men who institutionalized racism by what they said and did while forging a great democracy. It wasn't that men like Washington, Jefferson and Madison were evil creatures. Without their idealism, courage and personal sacrifices there probably wouldn't be a United States of America. Though they expressed misgivings about slavery, they nevertheless believed that blacks were inherently inferior to white men, and that the two races weren't meant to mix as equals in any society. Over the years this belief has evolved into a national attitude that has taken on addictive qualities. Even some of today's most enlightened citizens have been unable to free themselves of this social addiction, this disease that has produced a defect in the American psyche. Sadly, what keeps them from correcting the defect is refusal to acknowledge openly that it exists. Not only is trying to hide the truth an impossible task – it is a painful process that erodes moral fiber, produces guilt, and, in time, destroys societies.

In 1835, the French social philosopher, Alexis de Tocqueville, visited America and observed that whites and blacks were "two foreign communities" within the same land. In 1944, Swedish sociologist Gunnar Myrdal studied the racial landscape and concluded in his book, *An American Dilemma*, that blacks could not escape the caste condition into which they were born.

There have been changes in America's racial landscape since 1835 and 1944, but not the fundamental changes that are needed to turn the two foreign communities that still exist in our land into a single, truly united community. And, when you visit the black communities of America and study their condition, you can't help but conclude that most African-Americans haven't escaped the caste condition they were born into.

151

The situation prompted Malcolm X to say, "In America, there are 20 million black people, all of whom are in prison. You don't have to be in Sing Sing to be in prison. If you're born in America with a black skin, you're born in prison."

Across our vast land there are some individuals and a few institutions that are doing wonderful work in overcoming the devastating effect that racism has had on its victims. I have had the honor of meeting some of these unsung heroes. Others I have only heard about. Their self-sacrificing efforts have inspired me to continue what I have been doing for the cause of racial unity.

Naomi Oden was a black woman who had healed her wounds. She understood how important that was – and not only for her own well-being – for her own experience helped her to become an instrument of healing for black youths in Detroit's inner city. She could identify with their pain. As a result, she was trusted by those she tried to help. They weren't ashamed to come to her with their problems.

Her healing campaign was consistent. It continued with equal vigor during good and bad economic times. When her real estate business flourished, she turned her mansion into an unofficial human development center. During a serious business slump, she was forced to move into a much smaller house; but that didn't force her to cut back on her healing campaign.

Naomi started her human development work in the 1950s, when there were no government-financed programs, when there were no Institutes for the Healing of Racism and when racial segregation wasn't contested nationally. She saw a need in her community, and, with her own money, met that need well, oftentimes displaying a courage that inspired the youth she was working with.

Dr. Richard Thomas, who was one of those youths, and who is presently a professor at Michigan State University, recalls how involved she would become in her efforts to save the lives of the young men and women she was working with:

"She had a sixth sense as to when she should step into a discussion that was about to result in a fist fight. It didn't matter how big the guys were. This tiny woman would stand between them and calmly help them settle their differences. She shared her wisdom by what she did as well as what she said.

"A strong believer in the oneness of humankind, she made sure that we got to know whites on a heart-to-heart level. It was through Naomi that many of us were able to overcome our hatred and suspicions of white folks.

"Scores of black inner-city youth were the beneficiaries of Naomi Oden's human development enterprise. I don't know what would have happened to me if it wasn't for her."

I met Ross Hobbs when I was invited to Selma, Alabama, to help a group of black and white Bahá'ís set up an Institute for the Healing of Racism. Ross wasn't a Bahá'í, and didn't show up at the Institute formation meeting – yet, my meeting him was the highlight of my trip to Selma. I got to meet this white Southern man with a pronounced Alabama accent through a mutual friend whose children attended the school where Ross is the principal. My friend, who knew of my interest in education, insisted I meet his children's principal. He said that when his family left Maryland for Selma, he and his wife were worried about the kind of schooling their children would experience in the South.

"Our children," my friend said, "are ecstatic about their new school. They're not only growing intellectually, but, for the first time in their lives, they are happy in the classroom. Ross Hobbs has created the kind of spirit in his school that fosters growth and joy."

Though I agreed to meet the principal, I must admit I wasn't enthusiastic about the school visit. My Northern bias toward the South was a factor. Dixie, I felt, wasn't noted for educational innovation. I was planning on a fifteen-minute exchange of pleasantries with the principal and returning to my room for a nap.

The Byrd School's entranceway exterior was rather ordinary. But inside there was something special. Almost every black and white child I saw seemed to glow, radiating a contentment and joy I rarely see in other schools these days. After my meeting with their principal I understood why the children were happy.

Ross isn't the typical head of a school – public, parochial or private. During dismissal time, he stands outside, wearing a battered black top hat and wishing the students, "Good day."

When I asked him how he was able to create the kind of learning environment that produced such happy kids, both black and white, he smiled and proceeded to share his philosophy. "It's simple. I don't believe in integration. I don't believe in segregation. I believe in love and beauty."

Ross works hard in turning his beliefs into action. He persuaded the city and the state to give him the money to revamp the school according to his specifications. On his own time, he designed the plans and helped to supervise the construction. Today, every class-room looks out onto a courtyard with flower beds, fountains and birdhouses that attract all sorts of birds. He created a miniature forest and marsh land with almost every kind of tree found in North America, which functions as an outdoor botany laboratory. The polished oak hallway floors glisten. On the light green walls of the first floor are pictures of black and white men and women who, through the years, served their community well. And the children know who they are. Black and white teachers work in harmony.

In the summer, many of them work on one of Ross's pet projects. He runs an ecology camp at the school. Though he gets some funding from the state, it isn't enough to pay his teachers and meet the other costs, so he must charge a small fee. Despite having to operate on a tight budget, he'll never turn down a child who wants to attend the camp.

"Somehow we find the money," he said.

"Through studying butterflies and flowers together and going on field trips, the black and white children forget about racial differ-ences. They create a bonding spirit based on mutual respect – and love. To me, that is more meaningful than learning to recite some philosopher's speech on brotherhood."

After the tour of his school, Ross invited me to his home, where

154

we spent at least two hours discussing various metaphysical themes. He is a devout Episcopalian.

When I left Selma, the site of one of the meanest clashes between civil rights supporters and the state police in the 1960s, I thought of Dr. Martin Luther King who led the freedom marchers that day. But it wasn't what he did that day that came to mind. I thought of his "I have a dream" speech, which he shared with the world on the steps of the Lincoln Memorial in 1963. Ross Hobbs, I thought, was helping to fulfill Dr. King's dream.

Arthur Serota also has a magnificent dream: He would like to see schools established that would repair the damage done to black and Latino males by our public school systems. Arthur didn't wait for a miracle; he created one.

A lot of people thought he was crazy when he quit his lucrative law practice in Springfield, Massachusetts, to start the Learning Tree School. With some of his own money, a small grant and a few donations from friends, he purchased, in the heart of the black ghetto, a big, old house, which needed considerable repair.

The primary objective of the school is to prepare students who quit high school to succeed either in college or in the work field. Arthur bristles when his students are labeled dropouts. "These young men didn't drop out, they were forced out of school by a system that was insensitive to their real needs," he says. "These kids were capable of learning."

Arthur has proven his point. With an accurate understanding of his students' psychological and sociological background, he has drafted a curriculum which has achieved positive results. Every subject the students take is related to the real world. Before explaining an assignment, he is careful to point out how the assignment will benefit the students. With that type of guidance, he helps them create a career map.

The first practical objective for his students is passing the GED

155

exam, which would give them high school graduate status. Most pass it on the first try.

Special entrance arrangements have been made with local colleges and several predominantly black colleges in the South for Learning Tree School graduates. Those who opt to further their education – and most do – enter college with a belief that they can succeed not only in graduating from college, but in becoming whatever they want to be professionally. Before their Learning Tree experience, they never harbored such a belief, even though they tried to give the impression that they did. In 1992, more than twenty Learning Tree graduates entered college.

To achieve that attitudinal change, Arthur works hard in building up the students' self-esteem. One important way of doing that is to acquaint them with their rich cultural heritage. Because of Learning Tree's success in reconstructing the lives of young men who seemed doomed to fail, people in the ghetto have become protective of the school, viewing it as a star of hope in the community.

The young men are not only strengthened academically, they grow morally as well. Not through preaching, but through deeds – with Arthur setting the example. Since most of them have their meals at school, they help Arthur prepare and serve the food. They're also responsible for cleaning the house. Through these exercises, young men who once only cared about their own interests learn to be more cooperative, more considerate of other people's feelings and they develop an appreciation for community unity.

Arthur would like to see Learning Tree schools established in other parts of the city, as well as in other cities where many black students are pushed out of the public school system.

What individuals like Naomi Oden, Ross Hobbs and Arthur Serota have been able to accomplish takes a sense of selflessness, a spirit of generosity and a special commitment to service that's rarely displayed these days. While we marvel over their achievements, most of us don't really understand what motivates them to do what they do. However, those who benefit from their services do. Many of the beneficiaries are inspired to pursue a life of service of their own.

Noble, self-sacrificing public service endeavors by individuals and groups to rescue the victims of racism should be wholeheartedly supported and encouraged. However, their accomplishments cannot make up for all of the severe human damage that racism has wrought over the years. While we win some skirmishes, we continue to lose the war. Missionary-type enterprises in particular localities won't do what's required in overcoming so vast and deeply entrenched a disease as racism. Albert Schweitzer's heroic efforts in West Africa did little to change the social, economic and spiritual conditions in the region of the continent where he served for so many years.

In a sense, overcoming racism is like treating a rash of boils. After one boil is successfully drained, five others may break out, and the infection continues until the cause is discovered and a proper remedy devised and applied. Throughout our history, human rights advocates have been treating the symptoms of the disease of racism, but not the cause.

Racism in America is an old epidemic. It is so old that most Americans are unaware of being victims.

The symptoms over the years have become a natural part of our attitude, our behavior; racism has become a permanent part of our personality and national culture. Our awareness of the disease is relegated to its extreme manifestations – like the activities of the Ku Klux Klan. But, as I have tried to explain in earlier sections of the book, practically everyone in America is either infected or affected by the disease, including even some of the most ardent champions of human rights.

In order to begin a collective cure, the citizenry must come to terms with the true nature of racism, recognizing that it is a disease. We must understand how it came into being; must acknowledge – and I know this is difficult for most of us to accept – that ours is a racist society; that we have all been infected or wounded by it; and that we must develop ways to heal ourselves and the rest of the community. We must heal together – in our neighborhoods, in our schools, where we work, in our houses of worship, in our city councils, police departments, judiciary systems and legislatures. Employing the Institute for the Healing of Racism's method would be one way to heal. Hopefully, other methods would be developed.

Our nation's leadership must join in the nationwide effort to wipe out the epidemic, not through a series of symbolic gestures, but as committed partners, willing to draw upon every resource at their disposal to win the war against racism.

Because of the magnitude of the disease, and the destruction and havoc it has caused over the years, the leadership must approach its responsibility as if the nation's security were in mortal danger.

Can we do it? I think we can, because I hate to contemplate what will happen if we don't.

I'm optimistic, because, as I travel across our land, I sense an awakening to a need to do something that has never been done before in addressing the racism issue. There are signs of a willingness in some quarters to face the truth as to the origin and nature of racism. Though not reaching ground swell proportions, the signs are appearing where they never appeared before.

It is a positive sign that so many different kinds of people are attracted to the concept of the Institute for the Healing of Racism. They are stepping forward, revealing that they are infected and asking for help. To the wounded, that is an encouraging sign. For some, it reverses their drift to black separatism. It is a process that's underway.

I'm optimistic because of the healing that's beginning to happen. I see it first hand. I hear about it from excited women and men who are experiencing it.

Several days after speaking to a meeting called by the Interfaith Council of Amherst, Massachusetts, I received a letter from a minister who felt compelled to share with me what was very important to him – a sign of his healing:

> Dear Nate,
>
> This morning when I woke up, the vibrations from last night's meeting were still reverberating within. Thank you for the forthright and simple way you shared your vision from the heart.
>
> For some time now I have been carrying a similar hope in my head but lo, it takes courage to let it enter into one's heart. Your sharing last night shook another piece of it loose and helped me stand with a little more certainty on the only ground that I could ever call home within me.
>
> I think the times are ripe for an institute to be formed in Amherst. I perceive that the ground is shifting beneath the faith traditions. It is my hope and prayer that we are slowly finding a more unitive voice...

W hen people are exposed to the truth of racism, especially when they find out how it affects people – black and white – many of them recognize the need for personal transformation, and seek help right away. Barriers built by years of prejudice crumble. This was dramatically revealed to me, and to those who attended my lecture at Virginia's James Madison University in November 1990. It was an experience I'll never forget.

It was a small auditorium, seating about two hundred people. Most of the seats were occupied, and not by choice. Most of the students were there because their professors had ordered them to be there. The black students were congregated in one section, and the whites in a different section. It wasn't a case of following a university code. The students preferred to segregate themselves. When I looked into their faces – both black and white – I sensed suspicion, and with some, hostility.

The townspeople – old and young – seemed more receptive. I

guess they had come out that evening, because they were sincerely interested in exploring new ways of improving race relations in their town.

From the way they looked, the professors in the audience were there to judge my performance, to make note of any inaccuracies, and ask the kinds of questions that would demonstrate to everyone present that they knew more about the subject than the speaker.

It was a long meeting – much longer than I or those who arranged it had planned on. Four hours – from eight p.m. to midnight. Hardly a person left the auditorium.

During my talk I noticed the students – black and white – becoming attentive. In fact, they no longer seemed suspicious or hostile. After the talk, they had a chance to leave, but most of them remained riveted to their seats. They took advantage of the atmosphere of trust that had been woven in the place – to ask questions, make comments and share what was in their hearts.

A young black woman, who, I'm sure, had no idea that she would reveal her true feelings to white strangers, exposed her wound:

"I want to be a doctor, and I think I could be a good doctor," she said. "But at times I have doubts I'll make it, especially when I enter my biology class. I'm made to feel stupid there. All the fears I have about failing encompass me."

At that point she began to cry. It didn't take long before other black students started crying. Obviously touched, whites began to cry and moved to the blacks, and they hugged each other. I was stunned. There was nothing I could say, for there was nothing anyone could say that was more profound, more heart-stirring, than the expression of hope that was unfolding before my eyes at that moment.

But there was more. A young white student from Arkansas, with blond hair and blue eyes, approached me in tears. After embracing me, he leaned his head on my shoulder and said, "I never knew the pain before, I never knew the pain. Help me! Please, help me!"

There is hope. Certainly not the kind that stems from wishful thinking. Or denial. What happened at that James Madison University gathering provides us with a glimpse of what can happen if blacks and whites are exposed to the truth about racism.

But how the truth was presented was also a factor in generating the positive reception from a basically skeptical audience. What changed their attitude?

They sensed that I had no hidden agenda, that I wasn't trying to promote myself or a particular ideology. As the evening progressed, they knew that, like them, I wasn't cured of the disease that affects us all one way or another. They could identify with my pain; and because of that, some developed the desire and courage to begin healing their own infection or wound.

What everyone experienced that evening was the kind of sharing that takes place at our Institute for the Healing of Racism sessions. Watching long-standing barriers between blacks and whites crumble is like witnessing a miracle. Believe me – I'm not the only one who feels that way. Hundreds of Institute members across the country are enjoying the same experience.

Imagine what could happen if every community in America established an Institute for the Healing of Racism. Not only that, if every corporation, police department, school, college and church set one up.

What many of us believed never could happen, *would* happen ...

Appendix. Establishing an Institute for the Healing of Racism

Mission

An *Institute for the Healing of Racism* is founded in the belief that racism is the most powerful and persistent obstacle to the attainment of a just and peaceful society. An *Institute* recognizes the essential oneness of the human race; that all human beings share common ancestors; and that all of us share the responsibility to realize in our personal and social lives the oneness of humanity.

An *Institute* seeks to create an environment in which men and women of all races can address each other in a spirit of open and honest discussion, free of blame and victimization. The principle of trusting consultation, grounded in the belief that truth lies not in the individual perspective, but in the unity of diverse souls, is fundamental to every aspect of an *Institute.*

An *Institute* recognizes that racism is, above all else, a social and spiritual disease, a disease woven into the moral and spiritual fiber of society. It is born of ignorance and fear, which feed upon each other in a monstrous cycle. That of which we are ignorant becomes a source of fear. Fear itself breeds greater ignorance, which further magnifies fear, and so on.

The hope of breaking this cycle lies in the recognition that racism is a disease which takes little account of laws and statutes, but which reaches deep into the individual heart and mind. It is felt that only through addressing racism in our own hearts can men and women of all races generate a compelling power to eradicate this pernicious disease which so cripples our nation and retards its progress toward true peace and justice.

163

Purpose

To accomplish its mission, an *Institute* must foster an understanding of how it affects all people. An *Institute* is based on the notion that whites suffer from an inherent and at times subconscious feeling of superiority, and that ceaseless exertions are required to overcome this attitude. In turn, the suspicion harbored by people of color, resulting from a legacy of oppression, must also be addressed. An *Institute* faces these challenges in a sensitive and non-threatening manner.

Honest and frank dialogue involving all races must occur so that individuals may help heal each other. In the process, mutual understanding develops, which evolves into genuine and sincere friendship and love.

An *Institute* for the Healing of *Racism* has two major purposes:

1. To help individuals heal their disease or wound, and
2. To become a center for social action, whose aim is to foster racial unity within the community.

How an *Institute* Functions

The purposes of an *Institute* are ultimately inseparable. Neither can operate as a complete remedy, for the wisdom gained through personal reflection must be coupled with action in order to have useful results. At the same time, becoming involved in social action without embracing the therapeutic process could be irresponsible.

Since denial is a major obstacle, participants in an *Institute* begin with group discussions designed to help identify and understand how racism is manifested and how it impacts all levels of society. With this knowledge, participants become motivated to rid themselves of the main elements responsible for perpetuating the disease and retarding the healing of the wound. They become ready to attack the problem.

In a trusting atmosphere, individuals do not hesitate to share their true feelings. They feel comfortable, as their views are shared, not as a form of confession, but with the realization that they are afflicted with a disease or a wound and want to become better.

In this trusting and helping atmosphere, it is easy to recognize that an *Institute* provides women and men with an opportunity to make a sincere attempt to cure their sickness or heal their wound. The sharing is not only a way to relieve inner pain, it is also an appeal for help. When people of color reveal what it is like to be patronized or rejected because of skin color – treatment which in turn fuels deep-seated suspicion – whites gain valuable insights into the ugly effects of the disease. Conversely, when whites openly describe their struggle to conquer feelings of superiority, people of color observe a meaningful effort to deal with deeply-ingrained emotions. Members of all races respond to each other with appropriate compassion and support, founded upon unconditional love. In this way, an In*stitute* fosters a real attempt to destroy the root of a serious, pernicious social ill.

When genuine friendships are forged in this manner, the group evolves into a dependable force for social action. Armed with the knowledge of how hurtful racism is to a person and a community, members of the *Institute* become highly motivated to work to foster racial unity. Many *Institutes* involve themselves by promoting their principles through working with their local school systems. Others may choose another means of action for promoting social action. The key is that the *Institute* has galvanized its members into taking concrete action.

Suggested Topics

In order to galvanize the members into a strong and committed body, it is necessary for several sessions to be scheduled, at which time topics relating to racism can be discussed. No minimum or maximum number of sessions is required. Participants will be ready to suggest a plan of action when they have attained a spirit of love and harmony amongst themselves.

The following topics are suggested:

1. Defining prejudice and racism.
2. How racism is perpetuated – early childhood experiences, misinformation and segregation.
3. The pathology of the disease of racism and the nature of the wound.
4. Unaware racism – how we've all been infected.
5. Internalized racism – when the anger, hurt and frustration turn inward.
6. Stereotypes and how they affect us.
7. Institutionalized racism – examples of its presence in the systems that affect us daily – media, legal, school, health care, economics.
8. Oneness and humanity – achieving unity and preserving diversity.
9. Ally-building as a way to heal racism – an individual commitment.

Guidelines for Sharing

Sharing is voluntary.

We want to create a safe, loving, and respectful atmosphere.

Sharing is about one's own feelings, experiences and perceptions, etc.

We are not always going to agree, or see everything the same way, and that's okay.

Each person has a right to and responsiblity for his or her own feelings, thoughts and beliefs

It is important to avoid criticism or judgment about another person's sharing and point of view or his or her feelings.

Avoid getting tied up in debate and argument. It rarely changes anything or anyone, and tends to ultimately inhibit the sharing.

We can only change ourselves. Our change and growth may, however, inspire someone else.

Refrain from singling out any individual as "representing " his or her group or issue.

It is important to give full attention to whomever is talking.

Feelings are important.

We will surely make mistakes in our efforts, but mistakes are occasions for learning and forgiving.

We came together to try to learn about the disease of racism and promote a healing process.

We may laugh and cry together, share pain, joy, fear and anger.

Hopefully, we will leave these meetings with a deeper understanding and a renewed hope for the future of humanity.

Role of the Facilitator

Facilitators must be able to present both the purpose and format of the healing circle in a clear, concise and attractive manner.

Facilitators must be careful to set an example of the kind of behavior that they are striving to encourage in the participants.

Facilitators should find themselves being excited about the process of healing racism, and plan actions leading their own transformation.

Facilitators should act as instructors by helping participants look for key ideas and find implications for action.

Facilitators should carefully guide the group so that it functions within its intended purpose.

Facilitators must help individuals in the group reflect spiritual attributes, such as personal dignity, courtesy and reliability during sessions.

Facilitators should foster honest communication that is both tactful and constructive, and should themselves be good listeners.

Facilitators must accept in a non-judgmental manner the values and feelings of the group participants, and be able to feed back to the group in a positive, loving way what they perceive, hear and see without adding their own attitudes, feelings and prejudices.

Guidelines for Facilitators

Become familiar with exercises/outline before entering the meeting.

– What points do you want to bring out in the discussion?

– What issues do you think the group will bring up?

Arrive early to be abreast of any last-minute instructions.

– Create necessary seating arrangement (if applicable).

State purpose of session and begin with introductions.

– Give general outline of events to take place during the workshop.

– Be concise in your statements.

– Do some kind of ice-breaker activity to make group feel comfortable, at ease with you. (They will be somewhat familiar with each other.)

– Show enthusiasm.

Use listening skills.

– Listen for content and context of statements as well as affective level.

– Ask questions to check accuracy of what you're hearing: *"Do you mean?"*

– Paraphrase the person's comments in non-judgmental terms: *"Are you saying you never thought about white privilege?"*

Feedback is descriptive rather than evaluative. By describing one's own reaction, you leave the individual free to use the feedback as he or she sees fit. By avoiding evaluative language, you reduce the likelihood of a defensive reaction.

Be flexible and maintain some control of the group.

–   Do not let one person monopolize conversation.

–   Do not let one person get ganged up on, or allow a two-way debate between participants.

–   Draw the quiet or passive participants into the discussion.

–   Be assertive without intimidating.

–   Roadblocks may arise in the discussion. Use feedback at times like this. Highlight a group dynamic you see active; be open (yet selective) to sharing from your own experience. You may also want to circle back to a previous comment. People may still need/want to talk, but do not know where to go. In these cases relate their last comment with an inflection that makes it into a question.

–   Do not be afraid of silence. Do not put words into participants' mouths or succumb to the urge to steer them to what you feel is a right answer. Try and be comfortable with a participant's inability to be articulate about the point, recognizing, however, what the person has tried to say. Be affirming, supportive and directive where possible.

Leave time for closure.

–   Try to leave people feeling empowered to change rather than depressed.

–   Stress that this is only a beginning. Encourage them to seek other resources and continue working on these issues.

Some close-out questions.

–   What have you learned today?

–   What have you thought about in a new way this morning/
afternoon?

–   What concerns have challenged you? Can we brainstorm about
potential things to do?

–   How can we stay in touch to discuss future developments involving the diverse issues we explored today?

*Material for this guide was assembled from various Institute sources by Dr.
Mark Rossman, director of graduate studies at Ottawa University, Phoenix,
Arizona, and a member of the Executive Advisory Board for the Institute for
the Celebration of Cultural Diversity in Scottsdale, Arizona.*

Bibliography

Afnan, Abdu'l-Qarim. *Black Pearls.* Kalimat Press, 1988.

Bahá' u' lláh. *The Hidden Words.* U.S. Bahá'í Publishing Trust, 1939.

Bancroft, Frederic. *Slave-Trading in the Old South.* J.H. Furst Company, 1931.

Bennett, Leone Jr. *Before the Mayflower.* Penguin Books (Fifth Edition), 1982.

Berry, Wendell. *The Hidden Wound.* North Point Press, 1970.

Brandt, Allan. "Racism and Research: The Case of the Tuskegee Syphilis Study." *The Hastings Center Report,* 1978.

Capra, Fritjof. *The Turning Point: Science, Society, and the Rising Culture.* Bantam Books, 1982.

Chopra, Deepak. *Quantum Healing.* 1990. An audio tape series.

Conrad, Earl. *The Invention of the Negro.* Paul S. Erikson, Inc., 1966.

Dixon, Thomas. *The Leopard's Spots.* Doubleday, Page and Company, 1902.

Dyer, Wayne W. *You'll See It When You Believe It.* Avon Books, 1990.

Effendi, Shoghi. *Advent of Divine Justice.* U.S. Baha'í Publishing Trust, 1939.

Elkins, Stanley M. *Slavery: A Problem in American Institutional and Intellectual Life.* The University of Chicago Press, 1959.

Engerman, Stanley L. and Robert William Fogel. *Time on the Cross: The Economics of American Slavery.* Little, Brown, 1974.

Feagin, Joe. Quoted in article by Isabel Wilkerson: "Seeking Racial Mix, Dubuque Finds Tensions" The *New York Times*, November 3, 1991.

Fishel, Leslie H. Jr. and Benjamin Quarles. *The Black American.* Scott, Foresman and Company, 1967.

Gould, Stephen Jay. *The Mismeasure of Man.* Norton Publishing, 1981.

Griffin, John H. *Black Like Me.* Houghton Mifflin, 1977.

Hacker, Andrew. Quoted in "Apartheid: American Style" *Newsweek*, March 23, 1992.

—. *Two Nations: Black and White, Separate, Hostile, Unequal.* MacMillan, 1992.

Hanh, Thich Nhat. *Being Peace.* Parallax Press, 1990.

Howard, William Lee, M.D. "The Negro As a Distinct Ethnic Factor in Civilization." *Medicine*, June, 1903.

Hughes, Thomas, A. *The History of the Society of Jesus in North America: Colonial and Federal.* Longman and Green, 1910.

King, James C. *The Biology of Race.* California Press, 1981.

Kluger, Richard. *Simple Justice.* Alfred A. Knopf, 1976.

Kozol, Jonathan. *Savage Inequalities.* Crown Publishing Group, 1991.

Leakey, Richard E. and Roger Lewin. *Origins: What New Discoveries Reveal About the Emergence of Our Species and Its Possible Future.* Dutton, 1977.

Lowontin, Richard C. *Human Diversity.* W.N. Freeman and Company, 1984.

Madbubuti, Hakim. *Black Men: Obsolete, Single, Dangerous?* Third World Press, 1988.

Morgan, Harry. "How Schools Fail Black Children." *Social Policy,* Jan. - Feb. 1980. P 49-54.

Morrison, Toni. *Playing in the Dark: Whiteness and the Literary Imagination.* Harvard University Press, 1992.

Murchie, Guy. *The Seven Mysteries of Life.* Houghton Mifflin Company, 1978.

Pope-Hennessy, James. *Sins of the Fathers: A Study of the Atlantic Slave Traders 1441-1807.* Alfred A. Knopf, 1968.

Russell, Peter. *The Global Brain.* J.T. Tarcher, 1983.

Steele, Claude M. "Race and the Schooling of Black Americans." *The Atlantic,* April 1992.

Rutstein, Nathan. *To Be One: A Battle Against Racism.* George Ronald, Publisher, 1988.

—. *Education on Trial.* Oneworld Publications, 1992.

Thomas, Richard W. *Racial Unity: An Imperative for Social Progress.* The Association for Bahá'í Studies, 1990.

Williamson, Joel. *A Rage for Order*. Oxford University Press, 1986.

Wilson, William Julius. *World of Ideas, Hosted by Bill Moyers*. PBS Television, 1988.

Index